The Ecology of
WATER LIFE

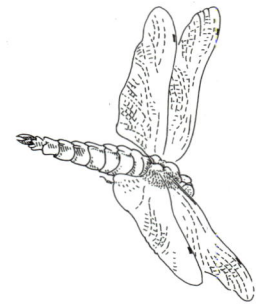

Franklin Watts Limited,
8 Cork Street,
London, W.1.

SBN 85166 448 2
First printed 1971
Reprinted 1978

Photoset in Great Britain by BAS Printers,
Over Wallop, Stockbridge, Hampshire, and
printed by Tindal Press Limited,
Chelmsford, Essex.

THE ECOLOGY OF WATER LIFE

by Alfred Leutscher

Foreword by HRH Prince Philip,
The Duke of Edinburgh,
President of the World Wildlife Fund

Illustrated by David Cook and David Pratt

FRANKLIN WATTS
London and New York

Contents

Foreword

by HRH Prince Philip, The Duke of Edinburgh, *President of the World Wildlife Fund*

There is a wonderful glamour and excitement about the great structures and machines of the modern world. Huge aircraft, ships, trains, bulldozers and great dams and skyscrapers have all got an overwhelming fascination. They only lack one thing, they are not alive. Created by men they cannot live without our constant attention.

As living beings we have more in common with what goes on in and around a small pond than with all the buildings and roaring traffic of the cities. We may feel very powerful and successful but the rules which govern the development and balance of species in the pond are precisely the same ones which control our own existence and future.

If man's activities are responsible for disturbing the balance of life or for the destruction of any species in the pond it is only a step before we disturb the basis of our own existence.

As people we are part of the living world and not cogs in the machines we have created. To look into the ecology of water life is to look at ourselves.

Introduction: What is Ecology?

ECOLOGY COMES from two Greek words – *Oikos*, a home, and *logos*, a discussion. It deals with the scientific study of animals and plants in their wild surroundings, and how they compete with one another.

A closer look at a plant or animal will show how beautifully it is fitted to its surroundings. We say that it is adapted to its **environment**. A fish in a marsh is built to move and breathe under water. A woodpecker is adapted to life among the trees, and belongs to a woodland. An earthworm is a burrower, and lives in the soil.

This adaptation to their environment is very necessary to plants and animals, if they are to survive. There are simply too many of them being produced every second, and if they all grew up there would be no room to move. As a result there is heavy competition going on.

In his famous book *The Origin of Species* Charles Darwin calls this "The Struggle for Existence". Only the successful kinds, or species, of plants and animals will win this struggle and go on living and breeding. We know from **Fossils** that many groups of creatures have lived in the past, then died out. Even giants like the **Dinosaurs** did not last for ever.

Today there are quite different animals in their place. This gradual change of living things, which has been going on for millions of years, is called **Evolution**. Species of plants and animals have come and gone, and new ones have evolved as the Earth has changed.

Once the **Woolly Mammoth** roamed in Britain when there was an ice age. Now the ice has gone, and so has the mammoth. Fossil fishes buried in the rocks tells us that once there was no Britain but sea in its place. Now it is land.

With each change in the surroundings living things have had to change as well, if they are to survive. Darwin calls this the "Survival of the Fittest". It is like a key fitting into a lock. In nature the "lock" is the surroundings into which the plant or animal fits, called its **habitat**. This could be a marsh, a mountain, a desert, and so on.

In each kind of habitat where an animal happens to live best, it can also find its food and reproduce its young. The fish in the marsh feeds on water plants, or catches small water creatures. It lays its eggs on the plants. The woodpecker finds its food, such as beetle grubs, in a rotten bough. It builds a nesting hole in a tree-trunk. The earthworm swallows the soil it tunnels in as food, and also lays its eggs there.

It is the same with plants. Some, like the primrose, live best in a sheltered place under trees. It is a woodland plant. The water lily grows in water as a marsh plant. The cactus can store up water and live in a dry place like a desert.

Knowing all this the **ecologist** can begin to understand how plants and animals are able to live in different habitats, and why life needs to be so varied. What he will do is to examine a piece of countryside and find out all about it. Is the ground soft or hard, flat or hilly, wet or dry, acid or chalky? All these things will decide what kind of plants can grow there.

For example, on some soils trees will grow and form a woodland. This habitat will attract the woodpecker, primrose and earthworm we have just mentioned. They are woodland species and this is their natural home. In a marsh they would be quite out of place. Such a watery home is meant for the fish and water lily.

Looking at nature in this way the ecologist can see how groups of plants and animals, called **communities**, are able to live together in one or other habitat. We speak of a woodland community, a marsh community, and so on.

Left to nature, all would go well with such communities. There might be a lot of killing and eating going on, but the community would continue to exist, so long as the habitat remained. Unfortunately, since we humans settled in Britain a few thousand years ago we have done much to upset the countryside. Where there were once woods and marshes and other natural habitats, there are now towns, roads and farmland. This has upset a lot of plants and animals, some of which have died out in Britain, and others which are very rare. They have no homes to go to.

However, not all is lost. Nature is very adaptable, and in a surprising way we humans have quite innocently provided new homes. For example, the gardens and parks in our towns, especially those with bushes and trees, are not so very different from woodlands. It is here, in the middle of a town, that you can see woodland birds and insects. The lake in the park, even a garden pond, is a bit like a small marsh, and will attract water birds, frogs and water insects. Such places are called **artificial habitats**, because we have *made* them.

The ecologist will not only study the animals and plants in wild habitats, but also in artificial ones. People living in towns sometimes complain that there is not much to study or see but this is wrong. Even the study of a rubbish dump or some waste ground can be just as rewarding to an ecologist, as a visit to some wild place far away from towns. There is always something to look for wherever you go.

ALFRED LEUTSCHER

SEASHORE LIFE

The Seashore

For most of us a visit to the seaside is a holiday. The seashore is also the home of a host of little creatures who know this world better than we do. Our footprints criss-cross theirs as we walk over the sand at low tide. Then the sea comes roaring up the beach and we are driven away. But they must remain, for this is their home.

In this narrow strip between the tides life would seem to be impossible. Twice a day, all around our coast, the sea moves up and down the shore. One minute it is flooded, and the next left high and dry. Yet life can exist in this topsy-turvey world. How do these seashore creatures manage to survive?

To find out we must search for them and see how they fit into this changing world. Some live on the rocks and stones, others in the sand and mud, and still others between the seaweeds.

Those living on rocks hang on tightly so that they are not swept away by the pounding waves. Usually their soft bodies are protected by a **shell**. The limpet, barnacle, mussel and whelk are made this way. When the tide is out, they cling to the rocks and close up their shells so that no water can escape. In this way they are safe from damage and their bodies are protected from drying up in the hot sun. They look lifeless, but they are very much alive. Once more the tide returns with a roar up the beach, and movement is seen as shells open to feed.

It is along the rocky coasts, especially in the rock pools, that these "clingers-on" are most common. You may find them also on the breakwaters and the pillars under the pier. This is where the seaweeds grow. They, too, must cling to something to prevent being washed away.

Seaweeds are primitive plants without flowers, called **algae**, which reproduce by minute **spores**. They have no roots, and many of them are attached to rock or stone by a stalk called a **holdfast**. The moist and slimy nature of seaweeds is due to a substance which prevents them from drying up when the tide goes out.

In these surroundings, tucked away among the plants, are other creatures which hide from danger. Crabs, small fish, anemones and many sea snails, do this, and wait for the tide to return. Most of our rocky coastline lies along the west and north side of Britain, in places like **Cornwall** and **Devon, Wales, the north of England,** and **Scotland**. There are tall cliffs with small coves and inlets in between, with plenty of rocks and seaweeds.

Along the **east** and **south coasts** the cliffs are softer, and there are many wide holiday beaches and mudflats, where there is plenty of sand and mud, but few rocks. It is here that many sea creatures disappear at low tide by burrowing. You can see the casts of sea-worms which anglers dig up for bait. Various shellfish, crabs, starfish and sea urchins will also hide away by burrowing.

In spite of all this clinging on, hiding away, and digging in, these shore animals are not entirely safe from their enemies, the sea birds. Greedy gulls and waders come down to the shore at low tide to search for food by probing in the sand and mud, and searching among the rocks.

The mudflats around our river mouths are favourite gathering places for the sea birds. Here they can find their natural food. Gulls which join us on the beach are probably after the food we throw them or leave behind. They act as useful scavengers, and will spend the winter inland, feeding on the rubbish dumps or following the farmer's plough.

Apart from these rocky coasts, sandy shores and mud flats, there are two rather special **habitats** along the shore which interest the **ecologist**. One area is where the wind has piled up the sand into hills, called **sand dunes**. The problem here, as we shall see, is how the plants and animals can find enough water and store it up in such dry surroundings. Even more of a problem is how to exist among the shifting stones of a **shingle beach**. This is where stones have been piled up by the waves, and worn into smooth pebbles.

Rock Pools

All around our coast, where there are rocky shores, pools of water are trapped each time the tide goes out. These are the homes of sea plants and animals which spend their lives there. No aquarium can equal the wealth and beauty of a rock pool.

The first signs of occupation we notice are the seaweeds, mostly the brown **wracks** which are anchored to the rocks by their holdfasts. Here and there may be a patch of green, probably the **Sea Lettuce**, or a long, ribbon-like **Oarweed** fixed to a stone. In the gaps between the plants, or attached to bare rock, are sea creatures which clench their bodies tight against the sun when the tide is out, but below water again become awake and active.

A **Limpet** moves slowly over the rock on its muscular foot, grazing on a lawn of soft seaweed. You can see its tracks where its horny tongue has rasped at the algae on which it feeds. It will return to the same spot from which it started, by the time the tide is out. Here and there are circular grooves in the rock where a limpet has worn a place for itself, so that its shell fits in tightly. Moisture under the shell will prevent its body from drying out in the hot sun.

Colonies of **Mussels** are a common sight on the rocks; they appear to be lifeless, but they, too, are alive. You and I could not possibly open a mussel with our fingers, but it has one enemy which can do this—the **Starfish**. Underneath its arms are many tiny suckers, called **tube feet**, with which it can glide over rocks. Clamping its arms onto a mussel it slowly pulls apart the two shells, then feeds on the contents by pushing its mouth between the shells.

Another way of catching food is to sit and wait. The **Sea Anemone** may look like a lifeless lump of jelly when above water, but below it opens out like a flower, spreading its **tentacles** which are covered with many stinging cells. Any small animals such as the **Shrimp** which brush past are paralysed

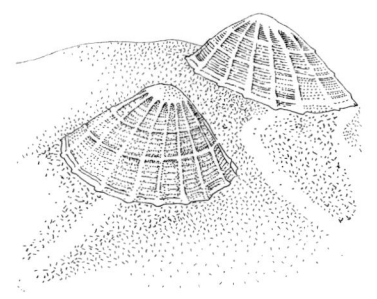

limpets grazing

by its stings and drawn into its mouth.

Here and there a **Sea Urchin** may turn up. It has a rounded or oval shell covered in suckers and spines. It is actually a cousin of the starfish and will also attack mussels and oysters. Buried under the sand or hidden among the sea-weeds a **Crab** may be lurking. It will scavenge any dead animal it finds or, if it can move fast enough, catch a live one with its pincers. Crabs are caught like lobsters by the fishermen who bait their wicker traps with dead fish and lower them to the seabed among the rocks. Because of its soft body which has no natural hard covering the **Hermit Crab** must find a ready-made home. It will search for an empty shell of a sea snail, test it for size with its claw, then pop it on. As it grows, it may have to find another larger house to wear.

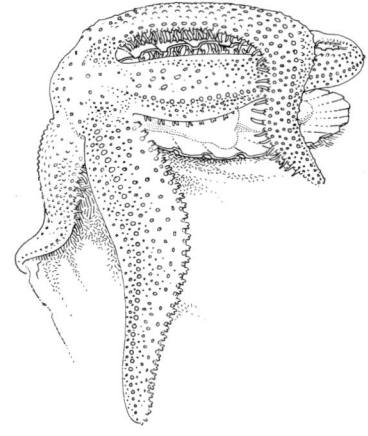

Crabs appear quite safe under their hard skins, yet they also have an enemy—the **Octopus**. Mostly found around the Mediterranean, the octopus occasionally turns up along the south coast of Britain. Shy and in-offensive to us, the octopus lurks behind a rock and uses one of its tentacles like a lasso to catch a passing crab.

Sometimes small fish get trapped in rock pools, but there is one kind which lives there permanently. The **Common Blenny** or **Shanny** lives around most of our shores and nestles between the cracks. If alarmed or caught above water, it can skip out of danger by using its large, rounded front fins as levers.

starfish opening scallop

All these creatures, and many more besides, share the rock pool all year round, taking up separate corners there and living different ways of life. This is as nature intended, for one of the laws of successful living together like this is that no two different kinds of animal can share the same food or way of life for long. Sooner or later one must give way to the other.

limpets

octopus

crab

hermit crab

common starfish

shrimp

common blenny

dahlia anemone

sea urchin

A

B

Two kinds of plumrose anemones

opelet or snakelocks anemone

The Shore Zones

Wherever the coast is rocky, there are many places to cling to and hide among, as we have already noticed. There is heavy competition for somewhere to live and the rocks are covered with seaweeds and animals. When the tide goes out, it is possible to explore the beach and to discover how this world is divided into zones.

As the tide rises and falls, roughly twice a day, the distance it travels up and down the beach gradually increases, then lessens. This happens over periods of seven days, and is due to the position of the moon and sun which are constantly "pulling" at the sea. When moon and sun are in line with one another, the pull is greatest and the tide rises highest. This is called a **"spring" tide**. Seven days later when the moon and sun are no longer in line, the pull is weakest. The tide is then at its minimum and is called a **"neap" tide**. Exploring the beach is best done during a "spring" tide when most of the shore gets uncovered.

Above the high tide mark is a **"Splash" Zone** which the sea does not quite reach, but which receives the sea spray. This is where **lichens** can be seen, making bright splashes of colour on the rocks.

Below this is the **Upper Tide Zone**, only reached by the "spring" tides. This is where the highest of the seaweeds, called **wracks**, are found. The **Channel Wrack** has grooves running down its fronds, and the **Flat Wrack** has a broad-shaped frond with smooth edges. Sticking to the rocks are patches of **Acorn Barnacles**. When covered by the sea, the barnacles open up to feed. The animals inside are lying on their backs, kicking food into their mouths as they sweep the water with their legs. Hidden among the wracks are **Crustaceans**, called **Sand Hoppers**, favourite food of shore birds. Small **Periwinkles** also live in this upper zone.

In the **Middle Tide Zone**, further down the beach, are three more wracks.

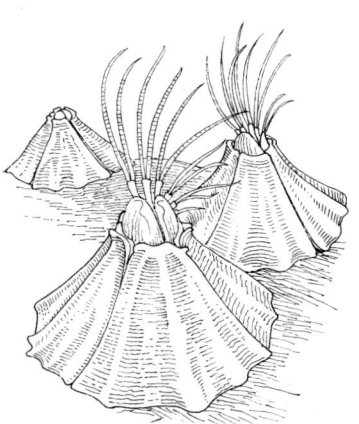

acorn barnacles feeding

The **Bladder Wrack** has well developed air bladders on its fronds, usually arranged in pairs. In the **Knotted Wrack**, look for the fruit bodies which resemble yellow-green raisins in appearance. The **Serrated Wrack** is easy to recognise. It has fronds with a saw-toothed edge.

In this zone will be found the **Common Shore Crab**. Its back legs end in a paddle shape and can be used for swimming. In the **Masked Crab**, the body is pear-shaped, with long antennae. It likes to burrow. Forming burrows in the sand are two marine worms which fishermen use to bait their hooks. The **Lugworm** is a dark greenish colour and the **Ragworm** more brownish. It has many bristles along its body. Two small fish may be found lurking in the pools. The little **Blenny** has large fins for gripping onto the stones and the **Butterfish** is elongated and more eel-shaped so that it can wriggle under stones and between rocks.

In the **Lower Tide Zone**, which is nearly always covered by the sea, are found the large brown seaweeds called **Oarweeds**, **Kelps** or **Tangles**. Some are straight and narrow, like flat, leathery straps, others more branched. Here and there is a **Red Seaweed** shaped like a palm of the hand with fingers.

Shrimps live among the kelps and are difficult to see when alive, as their bodies are almost transparent. Another **Blenny**, larger and more spotted than the last, lives in this lower zone. Clinging to the lower rocks is the **Slipper Limpet**, named after the shape of its shell. Colonies of them usually live together, one on top of the other. This is also the home of the **Scallop**.

This is only a small list of what you can find as you pass from one zone to the next. Plants and animals living at the top of the beach can stand more exposure to the sun and air than those lower down. Because life can adapt itself in this way the whole of the shore between the tides can be shared by a wide variety of life.

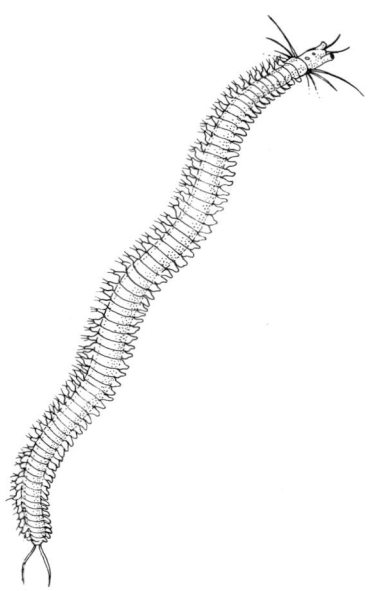

ragworm

lichen

channel wrack

flat wrack (floating)

bladder wrack

blenny

sand hopper

periwinkle

rough periwinkle

acorn barnacles

rag worm

SPLASH ZONE

UPPER SHORE
Only covered at high spring tide

MIDDLE SHORE
Average tide level

knotted
wrack

serrated wrack

red seaweed
(*Rhodymenia*)

oarweeds

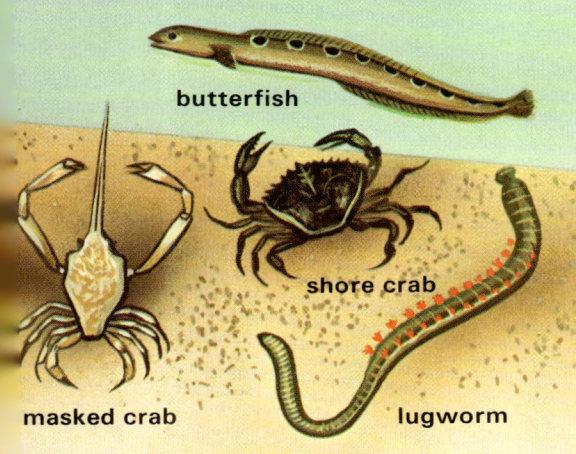

butterfish

masked crab

shore crab

lugworm

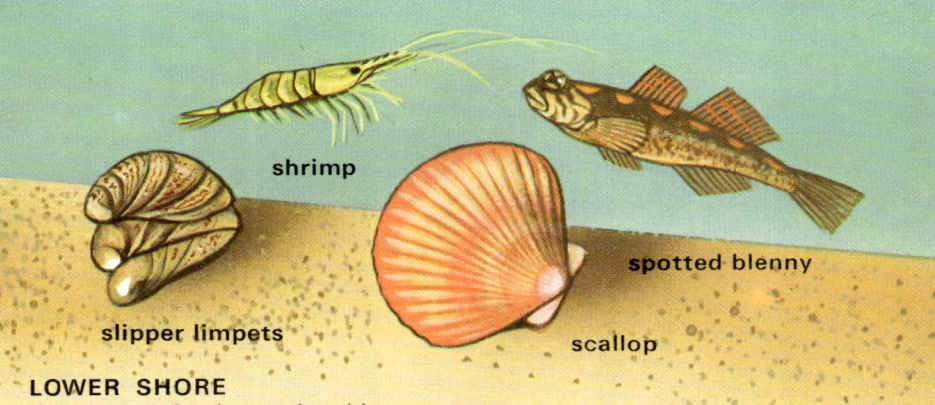

shrimp

spotted blenny

slipper limpets

scallop

LOWER SHORE
Only exposed at low spring tide

Cliff Birds and Plants

On the bare cliffs along the rocky coasts everything seems deserted during winter as the gales lash the seas against the rocks. By mid-May, however, all is alive and bustling with sea birds. Whole colonies of them are nesting on the ledges.

Best known of these cliff-nesters is the **Herring Gull** which comes inland during wintertime to follow the plough. It is a familiar sight on the beach during summer, and will follow a ship for miles in the hopes of a free meal. This gull is largely a scavenger, and will eat almost anything from a bath bun to a dead fish. At low tide it forages along the shore, searching in the sand or mud for marine worms and molluscs. You may even spot one dabbling with its feet in a shallow pool. This is said to bring the worms to the surface.

guillemot

Among the nesting gulls some dark sea-birds may be noticed. These are the fish-hunting **Auks**, black-and-white birds which dive under the sea for their food. The **Guillemot** has a slender, pointed beak. In the **Razorbill** it is more flattened sideways and has a white band across it. Both these birds nest on the ledges, laying their eggs on bare rocks. The eggs do not roll off because they are pear-shaped. Because of this the egg spins in a circle when touched.

razorbill

guillemot and razorbill

The comical **Puffin** or **Sea Parrot** has a gaudy beak which makes it easy to recognise. In spite of its clumsy build it is a speedy flyer and expert fisherman. Its nest is in a dark burrow. Sea birds, especially the auks, are somewhat primitive in nature's scheme and, especially when young, remind us of the reptiles from which they sprung. The strange growling and grunting sounds they make have given rise to many sea legends.

The largest of our sea birds, the **Gannet** or **Solan Goose**, is a handsome white fishing bird. It has a six-foot wing span, and glides over the water like a ghost. When it spots a fish, it will close its wings and dive in from quite a height, as high as a hundred feet. Gannets breed in dense, noisy colonies around our coast, mostly on islands. One of the largest colonies in the world is on Skockholm just off the coast of Wales.

How do these sea birds manage to find enough food for their young when they crowd together so closely? Being strong flyers they range far and wide over the water and along the coast in search of food. There is plenty for all. By autumn most of them have disappeared, the gulls going inland, and the auks out to sea.

Bird-watching along the coast can be very interesting, especially with a pair of binoculars so that you can see them close up. The best time for this is in May and June, when sea birds are nesting all around our shores. It is then possible to watch the parents courting, making curious movements as they shake their heads and hold them up in the air. Some even "kiss" with their beaks.

Where the birds are packed together in dense colonies a good deal of squabbling goes on, and sometimes a thief will steal material from a neighbour's nest.

A walk along the cliffs where the sea birds nest will take you among the wild flowers which are not normally found inland. A common sight is the clumps of **Sea Pink** or **Thrift** which manage to cling to the rocks. Sending their deep roots into the cracks they find enough fresh water and soil to live on. Another such rock plant which often grows on stone walls is the **Wall Pennywort**. It has an upright stem with clusters of green flowers on top and a circle of rounded leaves at the bottom. Another plant to look for is the **Sea Campion**, which has white flowers with a swollen base.

These plants prefer the sea air and rocks to grow on. Here and there are patches of **Lichens**, variously coloured in yellow, white, black and orange. They are seldom seen in towns because of the smoke and petrol fumes. A lichen is actually two plants in one—a **fungus** and an **alga**.

sea pink

21

razorbill

guillemot

puffin

gannet

herring gull

cormorant

razorbill

Shore Birds

As the tide flows back to sea, stretches of mud and sand are exposed, especially along the flat coasts and around the river mouths. At low tide these become the dining places of numbers of shore birds, such as **Gulls** and **Waders**. They search for the hidden worms and shellfish, probing with their beaks for something to eat.

The waders are especially adapted to do this. With their long, paddling legs they can wade in the shallow water, and use their long, narrow beaks to pick out morsels of food. Here and there you can see their finished meals, the broken shells of crabs and molluscs which did not escape in time. There are tracks everywhere which tell us which bird made the capture. Those with web marks between the toes are made by the gulls, and those which are separate, three-toed prints belong to the waders. Holes in the sand tell us where they have been digging for food with their sensitive beaks.

Waders are not brightly coloured. Since they nest on the ground, their dull plumage makes them well camouflaged. This is also true of the eggs and chicks. It is easy to pass by a sitting bird or nest without noticing it. One helpful way to tell the waders apart is to learn their different calls, a mixture of musical trills and whistles. Here are a few which you might watch out for.

One wader which does stand out very clearly on the beach is the **Oystercatcher**, also called the **Sea-pie** (from the old word "pied" meaning black-and-white). It has a bright, orange-red beak and pink legs. Its loud cry of "klee-eep" is a common sound along the beach. The Oystercatcher does not normally catch oysters, but is very good at knocking limpets off their perches and splitting open mussel shells.

Another common wader, the largest in Britain, is the **Curlew**. It is named after its lovely, musical call of "cour-lee". It has a down-curved beak and streaky brown feathers. It haunts the seashore and, when

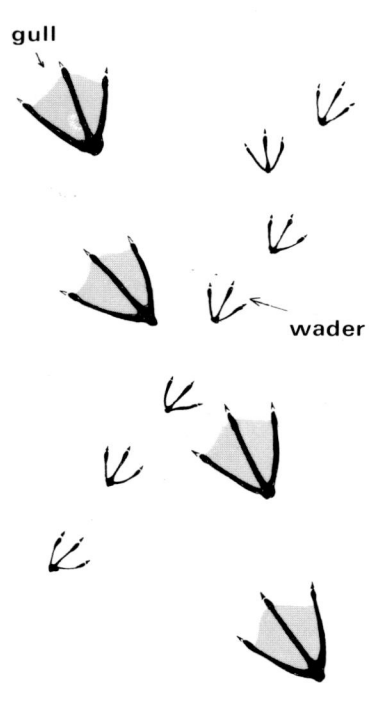

gull

wader

bird tracks

alarmed, makes a fluty, bubbling call. A whole flock of some hundred or more produce a wonderful sound of music. This is mostly heard during the winter months when curlews live along the coast. During the summer they make for the heather on the moors and hills to rear their young.

The **Bar-tailed Godwit** is another large wader, rather leggy, and with a long, straight beak. It has bars of black across its tail. This is a winter visitor, seen in large numbers along our northern shores. In spring it travels north to nest among the swampy bogs of the Arctic.

On the other hand the smaller **Dunlin** not only spends the winter here, but also breeds in summer on the west side of Britain. At this time of year its greyish-brown winter dress changes to a rich chestnut. This attractive wader has a dark patch on its belly.

We usually think of **Ducks** as belonging to ponds and lakes, but there are some which are found on the coast. The large **Shelduck** has a rather goose-like build, and is brightly coloured in black and white, with a chestnut "collar" around the front of its body. Being so conspicuous in the open, it hides away in a rabbit burrow to lay its eggs and rear its young.

The handsome little **Teal** is the smallest duck in Europe, only fourteen inches long, whereas the ordinary duck or **Mallard** can be as long as twenty-three inches. The teal drake is greyish with a dark head, has a white stripe above each wing, and an emerald green patch over its eyes. This duck nests in moorland bogs and in marshes, but in winter will come down to the sea coast and estuaries.

Many geese inhabit the coast during winter after their return from the far north where they have bred. The **Barnacle Goose** settles in large flocks on the salt marshes and meadows on the western side of the British Isles. It is one of the dark-coloured geese, having a black chest, neck and crown, with a white face.

tern silhouette

gull silhouette

greater black-backed gull

black-headed gull

barnacle geese

teal

godwit

oystercatcher

dunlin
(in summer)

dunlin (in winter)

curlew

shelduck

Sand Dunes

Certain parts of the coast are piled up with hills of sand instead of solid cliffs. These are the **sand dunes** which contain a community of animals and plants that can live in dry surroundings. Perhaps the most important of these is the **Marram Grass** which holds the sand together.

The stem, called a **rhyzome**, creeps below the sand, sending up tufts of long grass. If this gets buried during a sandstorm, a fresh shoot will appear at a higher level, so that the plant keeps level with the rising sand-hill. In this way a young or "white" dune slowly matures to form a "grey" dune. The change in colour is due to a surface of turf in which flowers can live.

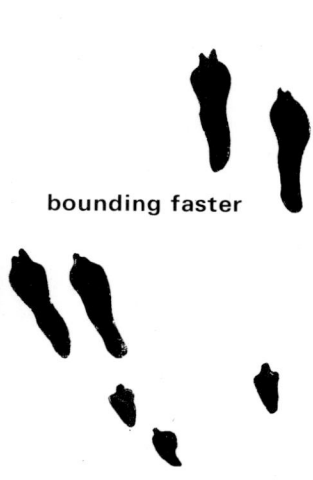

bounding faster

walking slowly

rabbit tracks

Since fresh water is scarce, and the rain soaks into the sand, these dune plants have ways of finding water and storing it up. They can also withstand the hot summer sun and the cold winter winds. Some have rolled-up leaves, like the marram grass, which cuts down the loss of water from the leaves. Others have a thick skin, like the pretty pink **Sea Convolvulus** which creeps over the sand. The **Yellow-horned Poppy** has a deep tap root and can even survive in the loose pebbles of a shingle beach. The prickly **Carline Thistle** grows close to the ground. So does the **Burnet Rose** which never grows tall. This creeping habit has an advantage. By day the dune is a hot and dry place. At night the heat rises in the air as the temperature drops, and this causes a heavy dew-fall. This is welcome moisture for the plants.

With plants to feed on, and soft ground to dig in, **Rabbits** often turn up and make their warrens in the sand hills. They attract the wandering **Stoat**, a blood-thirsty little hunter always ready to explore a hole. **Hares** are not unusual, and you may be lucky in finding a hollow under some bush, containing baby hares, which are called **leverets**. They are born above ground and are fully clothed. **Reptiles** with their scaly skins can live in dry places. One of these is the **Adder** or **Viper**, our only poisonous serpent. It is really a timid creature, beautifully marked with a dark zig-zag along its back. It never attacks first, and should be admired rather than killed.

One of our rarest reptiles is the **Sand Lizard** which needs all our protection. It can still be found in a few places, and you will recognise it by its brownish colouring marked with pale spots. In summer the male colours up a bright green. This lizard feeds on spiders and grasshoppers.

Many small creatures live in the dunes, feeding on the various plants. Some of these you should easily notice. The most common butterfly is the **Brown Argus** which lays her eggs on **Stork's-bill**. Sometimes it is joined by the **Common Blue** butterfly. The bright green **Tiger Beetle** is a fast hunter which preys on other insects. It ought to turn up near the back of the dunes where there may be some heather growing. Look for the bright yellow-and-black caterpillar of the **Cinnabar Moth**. It is nearly always to be found on a common plant, the **Ragwort**.

leverets

Always an exciting discovery on the open sandy beach is a baby seal. This is almost certain to be the pup of the **Common Seal** which has her baby on a flat shore, especially along the east coast. The larger, **Atlantic Seal** prefers the rocky beaches and coves on the west coast. When the common seal pup is born, the mother swims away to an island or sandbank and, soon after, the baby follows her to this safe place. However, if we fuss over the pup it may not move and could starve to death. This is why people are now warned not to go near these babies.

Life in the sand dunes is not so different from that in a desert, where water is the main problem. Unlike the plants and animals that dwell there, you and I are not so well adapted, and could easily get sunburned and thirsty, even become ill from sunstroke.

common seal

stoat

cinnabar moth

ragwort

sea convolvulus

cinnabar caterpillar

burnet rose

The Drift Line

Along the shore where the high tide ends are all sorts of objects washed up by the sea. Searching among this jetsam, called **beachcombing**, can end up with many interesting finds. Apart from the usual rubbish thrown overboard from ships, bits of driftwood, and the litter left behind by visitors, there are many dead remains of animal and plant life which belong to the sea.

Shells of many kinds of molluscs will turn up. Those of the **Mussel**, **Scallop** and **Limpet** are easy enough to recognise. There are also the shells of **Cockle**, **Winkle** and **Topshell** to look for. A collection of shells can be made into an attractive record of a seaside holiday, by placing them in compartments inside a glass-covered box. Remember to give the names of each shell.

Amusing little animal figures, can also be made by glueing shells together, and necklaces and bangles can be made by boring holes through the shells. A flower-bowl covered in shells makes an attractive ornament. The bowl is covered with one of the cement glues bought in a hardware shop. The shells can then be stuck on.

An easy shell to recognise is the **Razor Shell**. It comes in two halves which are sometimes found hinged together. The shell of the **Gaper** is more oval. Whereas mussels and limpets live on the rocks, the razor shell and gaper are burrowers. To do this the muscular foot pushes out of the shell, digs deep into the sand, holds tight like an anchor, then pulls the shell down after it.

Dead **crabs** will be washed up, but you may find what looks like an empty crab shell. This could be the outer skin of a crab still alive somewhere. Crabs and **lobsters**, like other **crustaceans**, shed their outer skin from time to time, even down to the legs and feelers. They must do this because the hardened skin does not grow. Curious objects, called **Mermaid's Purses**, are the protective cases of baby **Dogfish** and **Skates** which give

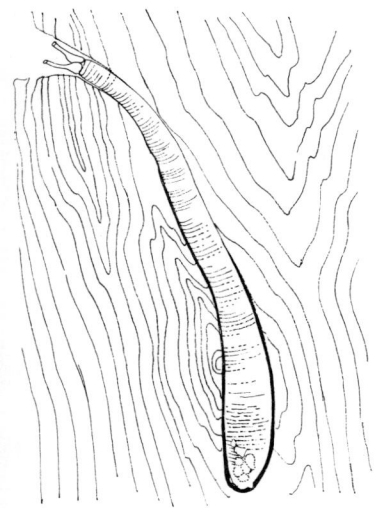

shipworm

32

birth to young instead of laying eggs. These cases are attached to the seaweeds. Inside a case a baby will feed and grow on its yolk until it is strong enough to break loose and fend for itself.

A round bundle of empty eggs looking like a bunch of dried grapes could be the spawn of the **Whelk**, a common mollusc which you can find in almost every rock pool.

A **Sea Urchin** or two may also be washed up as an empty, rounded shell. The common **Heart Urchin**, also called a **Sea Potato**, should not be hard to find. **Brittle-stars** are often stranded on the beach. They are cousins of the Starfish, with thin arms.

Since these dead objects are quite clean and dry, you could make a collection to take home, and, if you like, set up as a museum piece. Use a cardboard or wooden box. Cut away one of the long sides, and cover the bottom with some fine sand to resemble a part of the beach. Place your discoveries on this as if they were lying there washed up. Then, make a drawing or painting of the "seashore" you have created and put in the names of each specimen. You can then show it to your friends or take it to school.

Here and there you may find a piece of driftwood full of holes. This is probably the work of a strange sea mollusc, called a **Teredo**, which can actually bore into wood or stone. You may find holes in the rocks if you brush aside the seaweeds. **Teredo** is sometimes called the **Ship Worm**. It used to cause great damage to the old sailing ships by boring into the wooden hull. Houses on wooden stilts above the water have even collapsed where the teredo have been busy.

Have you ever found a bottle on the beach with a message inside? I have searched and searched, but never had such luck. A friend once found a wine bottle with a message inside written by a French boy in Brittany, and it washed up weeks later near Dover on the Kent coast.

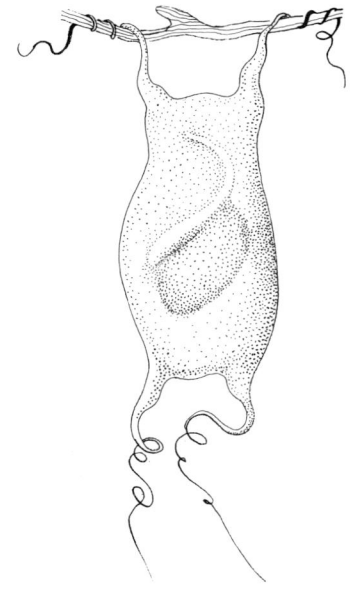

dogfish eggs (mermaid's purse)

brittlestar

oarweed

cuttlefish bone

mermaid's purse

scallop

crab shell

razor shell

mermaid's purse

mussel

scallop

whelk eggs

top shell

sea potato

Fossils

Buried in the Earth's crust are the remains of countless numbers of extinct animals and plants which are preserved as **fossils**. A visit to the seaside is a good opportunity to search for these especially where there are cliffs. These are really sections of the crust which may show rocks that are millions of years old.

Not all rocks contain fossils. Some rocks, called **igneous**, meaning fire, were formed during volcanic eruptions from molten lava and ash, and do not, as a rule contain fossils. **Granite** is an example. The best kinds of rock are called **sedimentary**, meaning "laid down". They are formed in water. Rivers which can wear away whole mountains carry down particles of rock that sink in the sea, and may finally fill it up. This hardens into rock.

Ammonites were creatures living long ago, having tentacles, and looking much like a kind of Sea Squid but with a curled up shell. These ammonite shells are sometimes called snake-stones. A similar creature, called a **Belemnite**, had a long, pointed shell, which people once believed was a thunderbolt that fell from the sky. Both these shells occur in cliffs along the Dorset and Yorkshire coasts.

Where there are chalk cliffs, look for the fossil **Heart Urchin** which is usually made out of flint and quite hard. **Shark's teeth** also turn up, beautifully preserved, and can easily be removed from the chalk.

Shells of different sizes and shapes turn up in many cliffs. One of these is the **Scallop** and should be easy to recognise. Fossil **Oyster** shells are common in a soft rock called **London Clay** which is all around the Essex coast. The **Isle of Sheppey** is a good place to visit. Here you can find the fossil fruit of a prehistoric palm tree, called *Nipa*. Looking much like a kind of flower is an animal fossil called a **Crinoid** or Sea-lily. Actually it

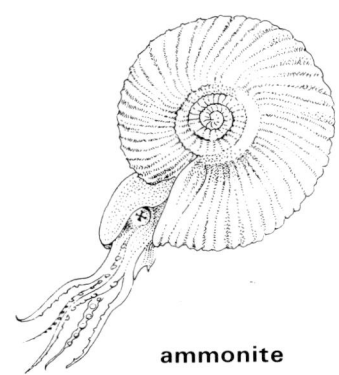

ammonite

is a kind of starfish which grew on a stalk attached to the sea-bed.

Limestone is a hard rock forming cliffs in places like Wales and Devon. In it can be found the remains of **Coral**, making attractive patterns on the water-worn rocks.

Other cliffs contain masses of shell animals called **Brachiopods**, or **Lampshells**. They had the shape of the lamps which were filled with oil in ancient times.

Giant reptiles which lived in the sea, called **Ichthyosaurs** and **Plesiosaurs**, do not often turn up in one piece. To find a complete skeleton would be exciting. Actually a little girl of 10, called Mary Anning, who lived at Lyme Regis in Dorset, found the first entire plesiosaur. Along the **Dorset** coast you can still find bits and pieces of these sea reptiles, such as a tooth or part of the backbone.

One of the most ancient of fossils you are likely to find, especially on the Welsh coast, is a **Trilobite**. This means "three lobes" from the shape of its shelly skin. An interesting thing about some trilobites is that they could curl into a ball when there was danger, rather like the woodlice in our gardens.

Collecting fossils can become a fascinating hobby. They tell us the story of life in the past, how it has evolved and gradually changed from simple beginnings to the plants and animals alive today.

Always remember the rules of fossil hunting. First, do not take any risks if you have to climb anywhere. Second, always take a companion in case you hurt yourself. He can then go for help. Third, tell the grown-ups where you are going. Lastly, before you go onto private land, get the permission of the owner. As a fossil hunter you will become a **palaeontologist**, that is, somebody who studies "ancient life".

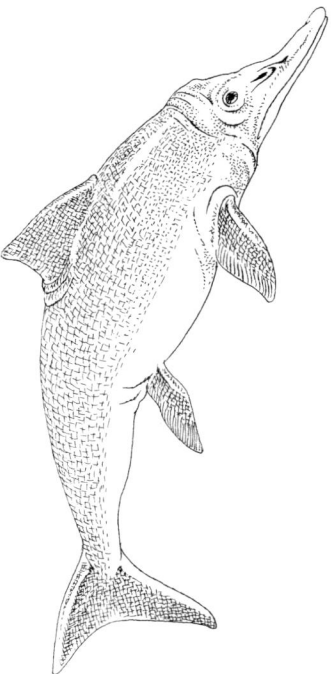

ichthyosaur

trilobite

brachiopod

ammonite

plesiosaur vertebra

coral

belemnite

crinoid

sea urchin

nipa

scallop

shark's tooth

oyster

Summary

Because Great Britain consists of islands there are many places to explore where the land meets the sea. As we have already seen, this varies from towering cliffs against which the waves are constantly beating, to wide stretches of flat, sandy shore. Where rivers enter the sea, there are mud flats and salt marshes.

These different shores are the homes and visiting places of the plants and animals we have looked at.

By **late summer** gulls and auks have mostly left the coast, and their place is taken by waders and geese that have returned from the Far North where they reared their young. The reason for these moves may have something to do with their food supply.

During winter the gulls have wandered inland to feed and scavenge in towns and on rubbish tips. Waders remain on the coast where the ground remains soft enough to dig up their food. Geese swarm over the salt marshes, feeding on grass. Together with swans and waders the geese travel north to places where the daylight hours are long, a great advantage when finding enough food for their young. In the rock pools life goes on normally, but at a slower pace, and is more a time of rest. Summer is the season for egg-laying and producing young.

A walk along the beach in **wintertime** can be quite interesting. Apart from meeting flocks of waders and hearing their cries you can see others who come down to the seashore, mostly looking for food. These are the animal "beachcombers", such as a party of rats I once disturbed. They were feeding on biscuits which had fallen from a broken box, probably thrown overboard by a passing ship. One another occasion I found some deer tracks.

Hares and rabbits will often visit a quiet beach, to feed on the shore plants. Foxes, too are not unusual, and are probably after the rabbits. My most memorable experience was the sight of an otter playing with some sea-weed in a rock-pool.

PONDLIFE

The Pond

Scattered around the countryside are many hollows filled with water. We call these ponds. Mostly, you will find that they are man-made. A farmer digs a pond as a drinking place for his cattle. Years ago the pond on the village green was probably built for horses to drink from as they passed by, pulling the stage coach. In the park or someone's garden a pond is built for ornament. Often when the workman have finished digging for gravel or chalk, the pit they leave behind fills with rain-water. I once found an unusual pond, where a bomb had fallen during World War II. The crater was filled with rain water.

Places like this are full of interest to an ecologist because they attract so much wildlife. At first a new pond, like my bomb crater, may be empty of life. The first signs I discovered were tiny plants and animals which can only be seen under the microscope. These are all around us, in puddles, and where water collects in ditches, cart tracks, even in our footprints. Such microscopic life gets blown about by wind or is carried on the feet of water birds.

From time to time, especially in warm weather, pond water may turn green. This also happens in a newly filled aquarium. It is due to the masses of minute plants which grow, called **Algae**. Tiny animals may then appear to feed on these plants. A common example is the little **Water Flea**, called *Daphnia*, sold in petshops as fish food. Such small animals become the food of various water insects like beetles, water bugs and dragon-fly larvae.

All these creatures were present in my bomb crater only four years after the bomb had fallen. By then **Frogs** and **Newts** had appeared to spawn. Water birds like the **Mallard, Moorhen** and **Dabchick** arrived from time to time, and the female **Duck** even nested. A **Heron** came once or twice to try and catch the frogs. One big puzzle was the **Sticklebacks**. How did they get there, unless someone put them in? They built their nests and reared a number of families.

Plants, too, grew up in the bomb crater and around the edges. **Duckweed**, **Water Crowfoot** and **Pondweed** grew in the water, with rushes, **Water Iris** and **Water Mint** around the borders. All this life might never have come together if the bomb had not fallen.

Wherever a pond is made, either by us or by nature, life will gather into a pond community for us to explore and study. It is even possible to build up a miniature pond indoors, inside an **aquarium**. Water animals, if properly looked after and fed, will live quite happily in this small home, even in smaller containers like plastic bowls and jars. However, before they are introduced, the aquarium must be prepared. The bottom is covered with a layer of clean gravel, or some aquarium sand (sold in pet shops). Water plants such as the **Canadian Pondweed**, **Water Milfoil** and **Water Starwort** are then anchored in the gravel with some stones, so that their roots can take hold. Next, fill the tank carefully with fresh water. Avoid tap water, if possible, and collect water which has been standing outdoors from a nearby pond or a rain butt. This will already contain the minute plants and animals which are necessary as food for your collection of pond animals. The kinds of food you should give will depend on what you keep. Some creatures need plants and others live food. *Daphnia* is a useful food, and can be collected from a pond by using a fine meshed net. Make sure the surface area of the bowl or tank is large enough to give the animals enough oxygen.

Depending on what you wish to watch and study these can consist of **Water Snails**, **Beetles**, **Dragon-fly** larvae, **Newts**, **Tadpoles** and so on. Always remember that any strong hunting creatures are going to attack and eat the weaker ones.

Keeping an aquarium is an excellent way of getting to know about pond life, and can be watched in the comfort of your home. When the study is finished, or the animals are no longer needed, they can always be returned to the pond.

The Pond Zones

As you get to know the life in a pond, you can see how it is shared out between the various plants and animals. Since the plants do not move around, each different kind turns up in the same spot, in one of the **plant zones**.

At the **pond side** where the ground is firm but moist, the water is just below the surface, so that plants growing there have their roots in wet earth. This is the **Marsh Zone**. An attractive plant which likes these conditions is the **Marsh Marigold** or **Kingcup**, a large cousin of the **Buttercup**. Some years damp meadows and ditches are covered by its golden yellow flowers during springtime. Other flowers to look for in this zone are the **Cuckooflower** with its lilac flowers, and the misty white clusters of the **Meadowsweet**. If the pond is on a heathland, that is, on acid soil, you should look out for an interesting plant, called **Sundew**. It has white flowers and a rosette of reddish leaves with sticky hairs which catch insects.

Beyond the Marsh Zone, where there is shallow water, the space is crammed with tall-growing plants forming a dense cover for birds to nest and hide among. This is the **Swamp Zone**. Every inch of space is used up because of the rich mud which collects. This is formed from the decay of dead plants, and soil which is washed in by rain.

Reeds and **Rushes** are quite common in this zone. Among them may be a patch of **Water Iris** or **Yellow Flag**, a wild relative of the garden irises. The **Reedmace** has small, dull-coloured flowers growing tightly together in the shape of a club at the top of a stem. When ripe, the fluffy seeds are blown away by the wind.

Beyond the bed of rushes and reeds is the **open water**. Here the plants grow entirely in water, and are called **aquatics**. There are three kinds. The **rooting aquatics** have their roots or **rhyzomes** buried in the pond bottom. By early summer long shoots have grown up to the surface, so that the flat

sundew

leaves and the flowers rest on the surface. The **Water Lily** is a well-known example, and the lilypads make a useful covering and shade for the pond animals during hot weather. The **Water Crowfoot** with its white buttercup-like flowers is an interesting plant. It has two kinds of leaves. Those on the surface are palm-shaped, but those below are divided into fine threads. In the **Arrowhead** there are heart-shaped floating leaves, and more arrow-shaped ones growing above water.

The **floating aquatics** have no contact with the bottom. They lie on the surface with their roots dangling. The **Frogbit** forms a ring of leaves with white flowers growing out of the middle. Side shoots are produced, like the runners of a strawberry plant, to form fresh plants so that a wide area of the pond surface gets covered. In fact, Britain's smallest flowering plants, the **Duckweeds**, often cover an entire pond so that it looks like a well-mown lawn of grass.

Finally, beneath the surface, are found the **submerged aquatics**. The best known is the **Canadian Waterweed**, or *Elodea*. Originally it came from America, and found its way into our canals and waterways. It grew so well that some of the canals were choked with weed and barges had great difficulty in getting through. *Elodea* is a popular plant in the aquarium because it grows well and gives off plenty of **oxygen**. You can see the bubbles rising to the surface when the light shines on it. A single cutting placed in the sand will soon form roots. Although it produces tiny flowers which rest on the surface on long stalks, these are rarely found.

With all this plant growth in a pond there is still room and shelter for the animals. On pages 10 and 11 you can see some of them. There are those that live on the surface and others at the bottom. Some hide among the plants and yet others roam about freely in the open water. We shall learn more about them later on.

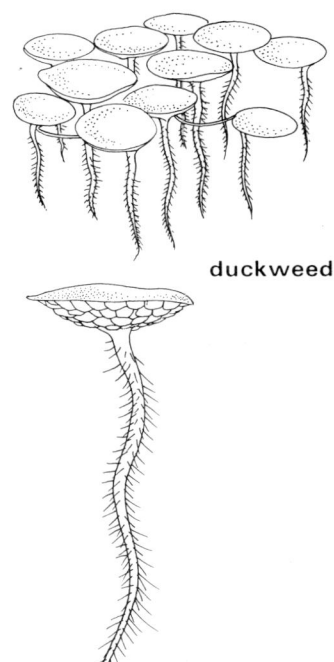

duckweed

marsh marigold

water iris

reedmace

arrowhead

MARSH PLANTS

SWAMP PLANTS

water crowfoot

fringed water lily

FLOATING AQUATICS

frogbit

SUBMERGED AQUATICS

FREE SWIMMERS

Canadian pondweed

HIDDEN DWELLERS

BOTTOM DWELLERS

ROOTING AQUATICS

Microscopic Pond Life

The places we humans can live in and go to seem almost endless, now that we can travel to the moon. There is also another world in which plants and animals can exist, in a space no bigger than a drop of water. Placed under the microscope these midgets appear in all shapes and sizes, busily moving about as they search for food, or avoid being caught.

Even the tiny plants are active. One common example is *Euglena* (you-glee-na), a single plant cell shaped like a pear. It pulls itself along with a thread called a **flagellum**. Large quantities of these plants can turn a pond or puddle green. This is due to a chemical, called **chlorophyll** (clor-o-fill), meaning "leaf-green," which only plants possess.

Many plants called **Diatoms** occur in ponds as well as the sea. They are beautifully shaped, some elongated, others starlike, and others more like a half-moon. Some move about slowly, resembling tiny spacecraft.

Volvox is a colony of plant cells living together in the shape of a globe which revolves slowly through the water. The outside cells have tiny whips, called **cilia** (sil-ee-a) which beat the water to move *Volvox* along its way.

Spirogyra (spy-ro-ji-ra) consists of plant cells growing end to end in long threads. Running through each cell is a spiral band of chlorophyll. It has a slimy touch and is sometimes called **Blanketweed**.

One of the most fascinating animals to watch is the **Ghost Animalcule**, called *Amoeba* (a-mee-ba). This single cell is held together by a thin elastic membrane so that it can change its shape. It creeps along by pushing out part of its body to form **pseudopodia** (soo-do-po-dee-a), a word meaning "false feet". *Amoeba* is sensitive to its surroundings, and will turn away from a bright light or from any pollution. It rolls into a tight ball when there is a drought and the water dries up. It can then be carried away on specks of mud by the wind, or on the feet of birds. To catch its food it wraps itself around the meal to form a kind of stomach. Juices poured into this food **vacuole** digest the captive. From time to time

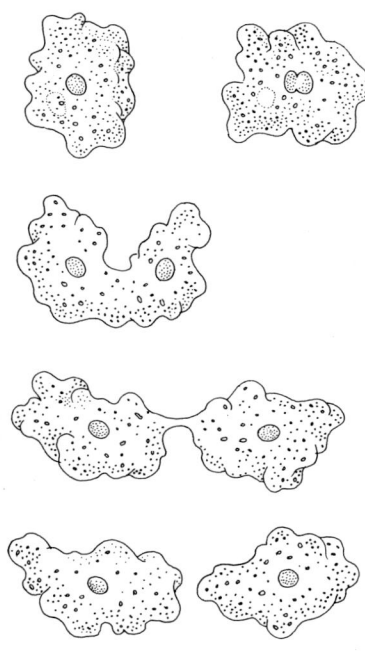

amoeba dividing

another vacuole forms and takes up any waste. This is set free when the vacuole bursts. Making a family could not be simpler. The *Amoeba* comes to rest, then divides into two!

Difflugia (diff-loo-gee-a), a cousin of *Amoeba*, also has false feet, but in addition builds a shell around itself. The "feet" can be pushed through the hole in the shell to catch a meal.

Paramoecium (par-a-mee-sium) is called the **Slipper Animalcule**, as it is shaped like a tiny lady's slipper. It is a lively little animal, covered in rows of cilia which beat backwards and forwards to push it along in a corkscrew fashion. *Vorticella* remains fixed to a stalk, and catches food with a ring of cilia around its mouth.

Apart from the above one-celled plants and animals there are some larger, many-celled kinds which can just be seen with the naked eye. One of these is called the **Water Flea**, or *Daphnia* (daff-nee-a). It is not really a flea—which is an insect—but a **crustacean** and related to crabs. In summer thousands of them can be seen jerking about in the pond in a flea-like fashion. A larger crustacean, the **Freshwater Shrimp**, is a favourite food of fish, especially the **Trout**, and lives best in slow-moving water.

Cyclops (sigh-klops) is a cousin of *Daphnia*, rather pear-shaped, and with long feelers. Its two eyes are so close together that they look like one, so it has been named after the one-eyed giant in Greek mythology.

Look carefully at any water plant you have collected, and you may find a little animal looking like a minute sea-anemone. It has a similar row of tentacles full of stings, and catches food with them. It is named **Hydra**, after the creature in the ancient Greek legend which had a head covered with snakes. Sometimes *Hydra* produces offspring which grow out of its body, and then break off. This is called **budding**.

All these microscopic animals are produced in enormous numbers, and are important to the pond community as food for the larger animals.

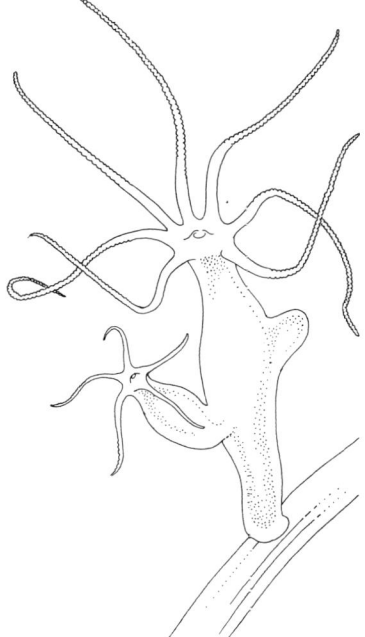

hydra budding

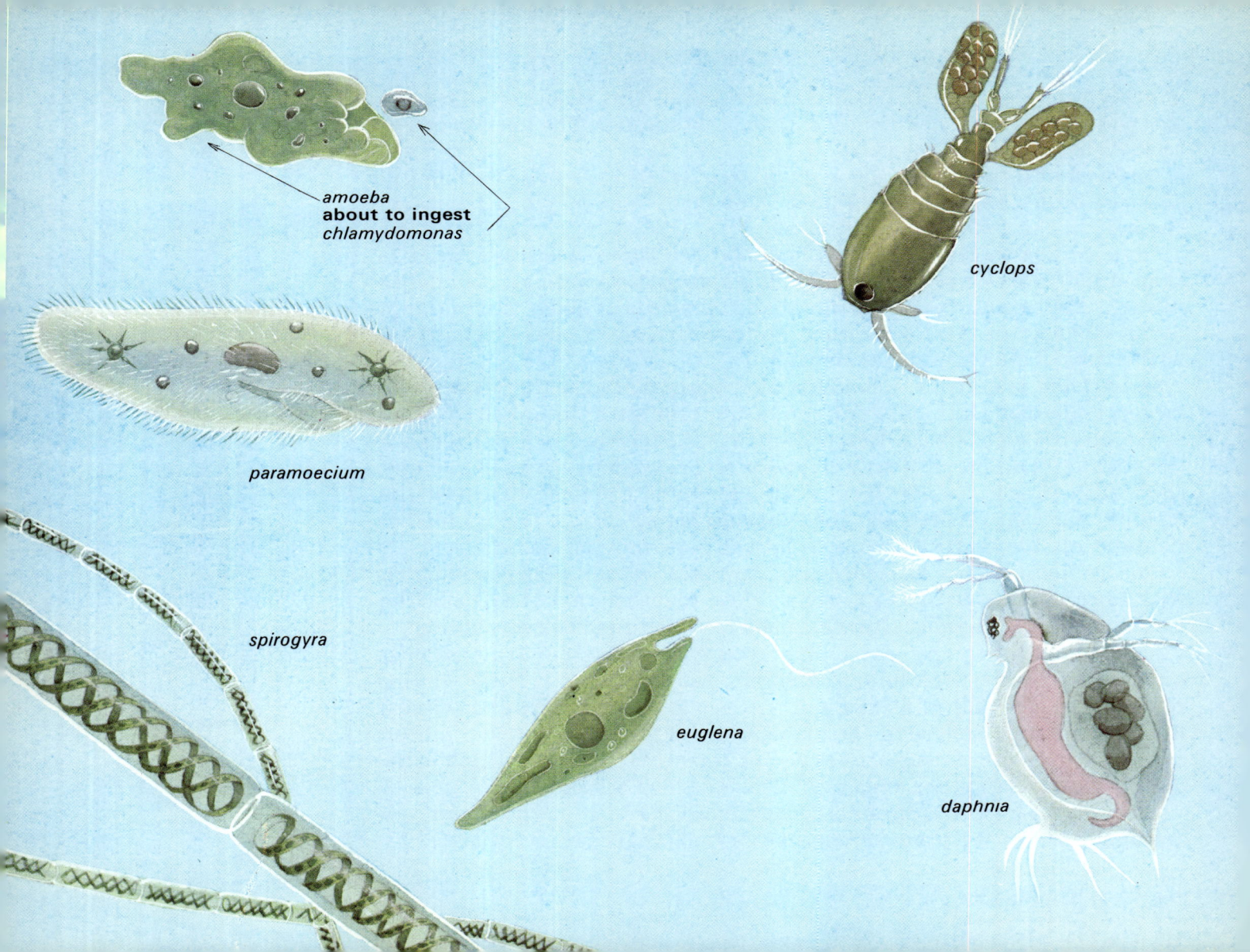

amoeba
about to ingest
chlamydomonas

cyclops

paramoecium

spirogyra

euglena

daphnia

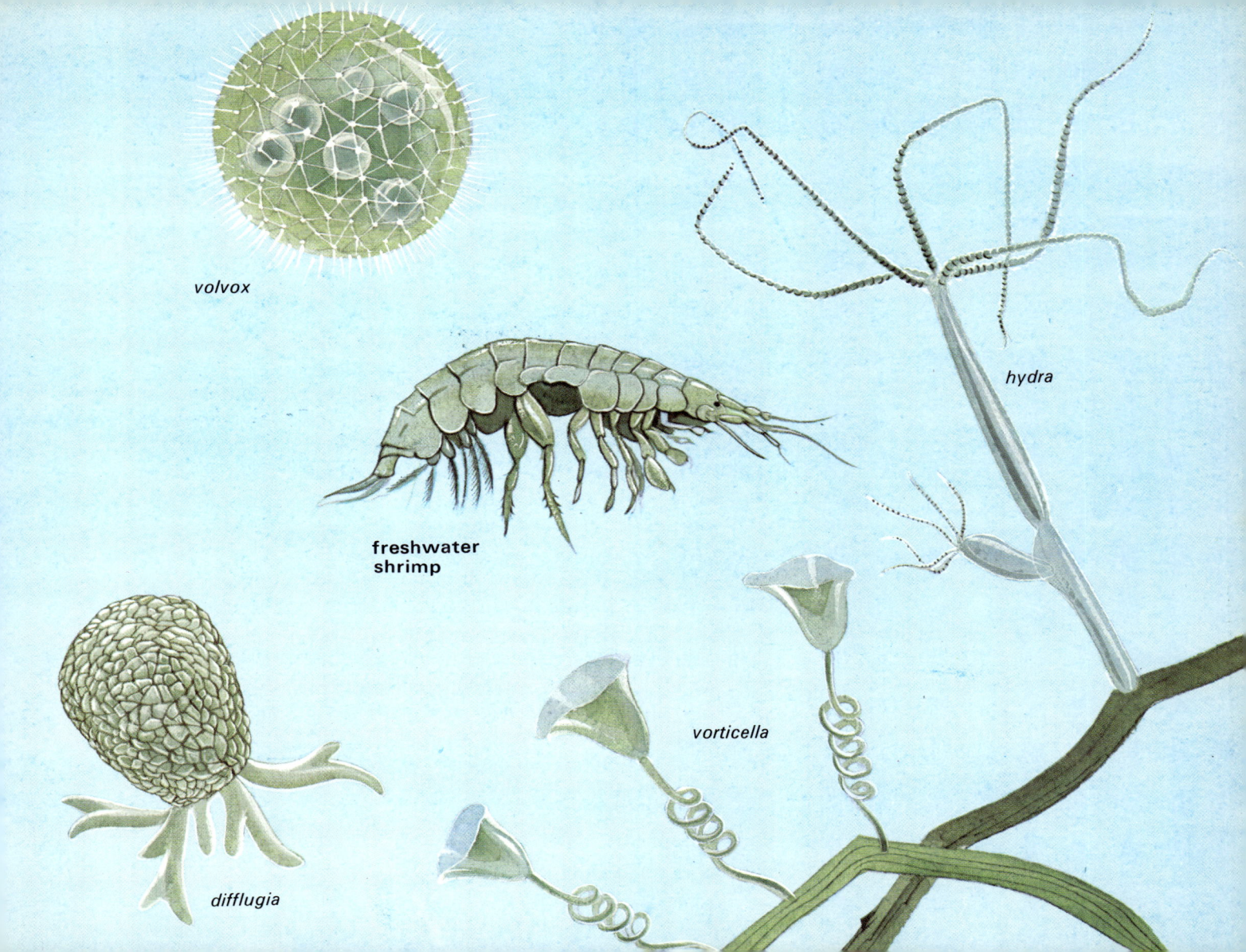

volvox

hydra

freshwater
shrimp

vorticella

difflugia

Water Insects and Others

Whereas most insects live on land, there are a number of them to be found in freshwater where they live or breed in ponds. Some like the **Water Skater** dart about over the surface. Others hang from the surface, and are the larval stage of various **Gnats** and **Midges**. Magnify one and you can see that it hangs head downwards so that its air tube touches the surface. It sticks there because of a very fine skin on the water, called the **surface film** which acts as a kind of magnet. Around its head are many tiny bristles which are twitching: they are sweeping the water for food.

The **Water Boatman** is a water bug which swims upside down. It darts about the pond using a pair of long legs like oars. This insect has a sharp stabbing mouth with which it can suck out the inside of its prey. If you ever catch one, be careful how you handle it.

Another water bug, called the **Water Scorpion** because of its shape, appears to have a pair of sharp jaws and an unpleasant-looking sting. What look like jaws are really the front pair of legs.

Hiding among the water plants it will use these to snatch at any passing prey, rather like the mantis does on land. The "sting" is only an air-breathing tube, and also used by the female for laying her eggs. The long, thin **Water Measurer** is another kind of water bug. The larva of the **Dragonfly** does not need to come up for air, as it can breathe underwater. It catches its food with a curious pair of jaws fixed to a hinge which shoots out after its prey.

Beetles are usually quite common in ponds. Colonies of **Whirligig Beetles** are easy to find as they spin over the surface in a dizzy fashion. They never seem to collide. If you disturb them they will dart under. Soon they are back, and carry on in their aimless circles.

One of the largest British beetles is the **Great Diving Beetle** or *Dytiscus*. About 3 cm long, a chestnut brown in colour, it is one of the fiercest of the

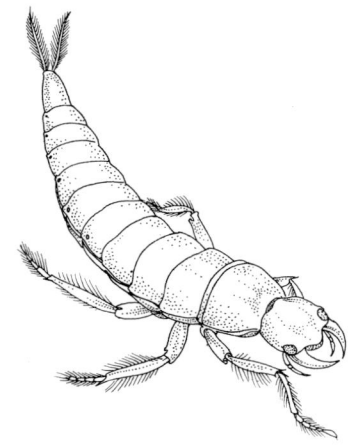

larva of
great diving beetle

pond inmates. It swims everywhere and will pounce on tadpoles, newts, small fish, and give *you* quite a nip if you pick it up. This beetle is best put by itself if you want to keep one for study. Feed it on earthworms and bits of raw meat. Even the large **Warty Newt** is not safe from this beetle. It lays its eggs on water plants and these hatch into long-shaped larvae just as ferocious as their parents. When fully grown, in about a month, the larva crawls out onto a muddy bank and digs a tunnel. Here it turns into a **pupa**. From this a beetle will emerge and return to the water.

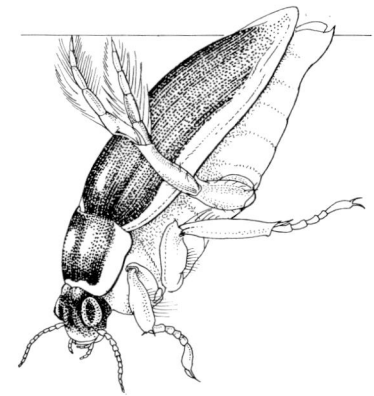

great diving beetle
breathing

Snails also live in ponds, plenty of them. They wander about on their muscular feet, browsing on plants and debris. Even some of these must come up for air. The large **Ramshorn Snail**, called *Planorbis*, has a shell shaped like the horn of a ram. In the **Great Pond Snail**, or *Limnaea*, the shell spirals to a point. They can actually crawl along the pond surface film upside-down. In this position the air chamber opens up to take in a fresh supply.

All corners of the pond are occupied. On the bottom, living on the mud or gravel you can see the tracks of the **Pond Mussel**. To move about it opens up its twin shell and pushes out its tongue-like foot into the mud, and pulls itself along. At one end are two openings, the **siphons**, through which water can pass. From this it filters off the minute plant and animal life on which it feeds.

One of the most interesting pond dwellers is the **Water Spider**, which also needs air. First, it spins a web under water among the plants. Collecting bubbles or air from the surface it places these under the web, which is then forced up into a dome shape. This is called the **diving bell**. In this the spider can hide, take in its food, lay its eggs, and even hibernate. I have even watched a spider build its home inside a jam jar after it was caught. It finished it in only half-an-hour.

raft of eggs

culex
mosquito

pupa

ramshorn
snail
(*Planorbis*)

larva

(foreground)
water spider
(background) bell

water
scorpion

dragonfly larva
catching tadpole

damselfly larva

water
measurer

water skater

whirligig beetle

water boatmen

great diving beetle (*Dytiscus*)

pond snails (*Limnaea*)

warty newts

female

male

pond mussel

The Stickleback

Of all the fishes which live in ponds, one of the best known, and also the commonest, is the **Three-spined Stickleback**, often called the **Tiddler**. You can catch it with a net and take it home to live in a jam-jar or bowl. Far better, if possible, would be to give it a larger home such as an aquarium. If this is properly set up with sand and plants, a fascinating story can be watched as this little fish goes through its breeding habits. The stickleback actually builds a nest for the eggs, and it is the father who does all the work.

By about May the males are busy in the ponds and ditches where they live. You can recognise a male by the bright red colouring on the throat. Each one chooses an opening between the water plants and, like the garden robin, will guard its territory. Even larger fish, newts, beetles and so on are attacked and driven off if they come too close. Should another male enter its neighbour's domain then a real fight begins. Circling one another, the two will attack by raising the two spines which are fitted one to each side of the body. Only occasionally do they hurt one another, and it is nearly always the rival that is chased away. If the winner then follows into the other's home, the position is reversed, and he gets the worst of it.

Soon the male starts to build his nest by tearing off bits of water plant with his mouth. These are pushed into a small heap on the pond or aquarium bottom. To bind the material together he will hover over the nest and squirt a sticky substance from his body. This acts as a kind of glue. The male even picks up mouthfuls of sand and scatters this over the nest to hold it down. Next, he prods the nest with his mouth to make a door-way. All the time he is ready to chase off any intruders.

Now it is time to look for a wife. The mature females are pale-coloured and plump with eggs. How can the male tell the difference from another male? The bright red throat is the answer. This has been shown by making model sticklebacks and putting them in the aquarium. The

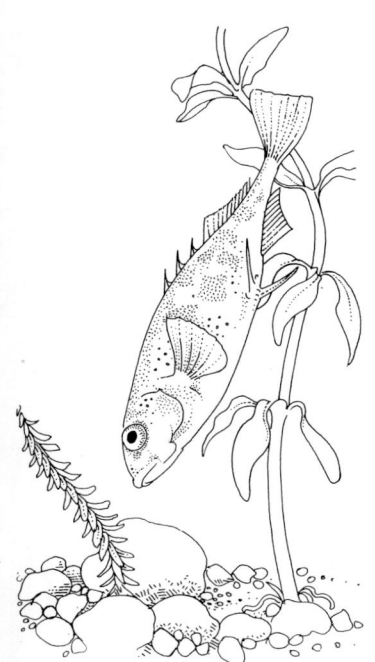

stickleback
in defence posture

56

model with a red throat gets attacked, and the plain one may even be courted!

A male will circle around a female in a kind of zig-zag dance from side to side, and slowly move towards the nest. If the female is in the mood to lay eggs, she will follow. She pushes her way into the doorway and wriggles right through the nest, coming to rest with her head and tail sticking out at opposite ends. In this position she lays her eggs, then comes out on the other side. In this way a tunnel is made through the nest. This is important, as we shall see in a moment. From now on the male takes no further interest in the female, and chases her away as if she were an enemy.

Now and then he tilts his body, facing the opening head downwards. By waving his body and fins he sends a current of water through the tunnel to cool and aerate the eggs. This is called "**fanning**". At last the tiny **fry** appear in a little shoal, and now father's troubles really begin. Not only must he fight all comers, but also watch the youngsters which may wander off. He will then gather them up in his mouth and spit them out close to the nest without hurting them.

Finally the little ones are old enough to fend for themselves, and father loses interest. You can see shoals of young sticklebacks along the pond-side during early summer. One day the lucky ones that escape being eaten will build their own nests or lay eggs for yet another generation of sticklebacks.

A male stickleback has one curious habit when warning away a rival. He will stand on his head. I remember once when breeding these little fish, how the male kept on doing this although there was no enemy in sight. Then I discovered it happened each time I approached. I was wearing a red tie, and I was the enemy! Another occasion I managed to get two males to nest at the same time in one aquarium. There were plenty of fights going on *that* year.

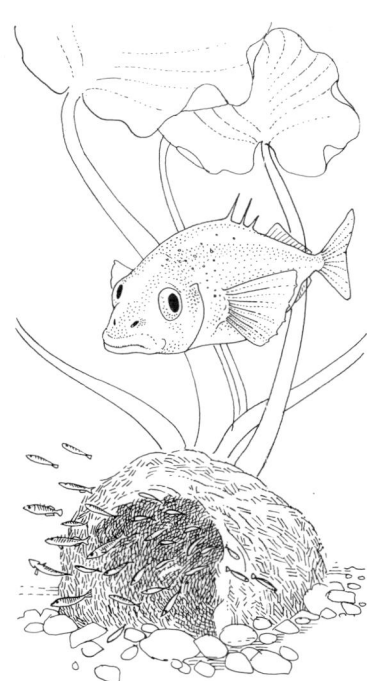

stickleback
looking after fry

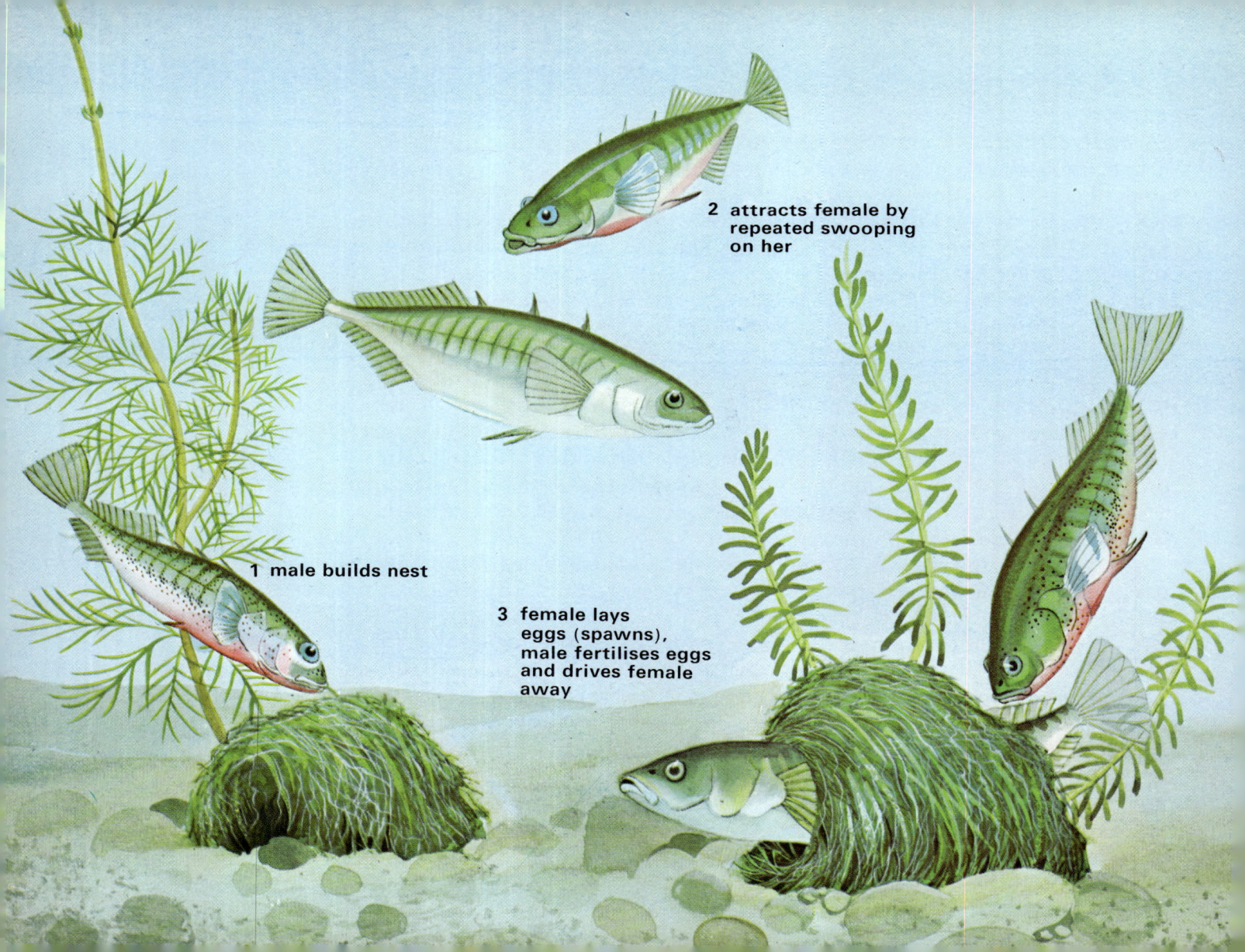

2 attracts female by repeated swooping on her

1 male builds nest

3 female lays eggs (spawns), male fertilises eggs and drives female away

4
male drives away
any intruders
near his nest

5
male aerates
water by using his
pectoral fins,
continues to shepherd
young when hatched

Water Birds

Around the pondside the tall reeds and rushes make ideal cover for a number of birds which nest close to water. Most of them will use the pond as a larder for getting their food.

Everyone knows the **Wild Duck** or **Mallard**. In the open countryside it can be very shy and difficult to approach, but in towns and villages you can get close enough to admire the beautiful plumage of the drake. Above its white collar the head is a rich emerald. As it turns its head or swims past, the colour may change to a deep purple. This is due to the light which reflects a different colour according to the angle you see it.

The dull-coloured female usually nests on the ground by the waterside, hidden in the undergrowth. She is so well camouflaged that you could easily pass her by. When they hatch, the ducklings immediately enter the water and start feeding without help from their mother. Occasionally a duck will nest above ground in the crown of a tree. I once watched some babies deliberately topple out and fall into the water below without hurting themselves. In towns ducks sometimes nest on top of buildings which have roof gardens. There is one London store where this often happens. Mother and ducklings then have to be taken down in the lift, and escorted across the road whilst the traffic is held up, so that they can reach the lake in the nearby park!

When the parents have finished nesting, they **moult**. The wing feathers come out in bunches, so that the ducks cannot fly. Since he might look too conspicuous on the ground, the drake changes his plumage for a few weeks to look like the female. This is called the **eclipse plumage**.

The Mallard is a surface duck, and does not normally go under water but upends its body to search for food. A black and white duck you may see on a pond, which has a crest on its head, is probably the **Tufted Duck**. The female is more brownish. This is one of the diving ducks which often bobs underwater to collect food at the bottom.

Another diver is the **Pochard**. The drake has a greyish body with a black chest, and a chestnut head and neck. Here again the female is dull in

little grebe and nest

60

colour. This is a common rule with ducks, since they nest on the ground, and the female does not want to give herself away with bright colours.

Ducks often swim in open water, whereas the **Moorhen** usually lurks among the reeds and rushes. It is easy to recognise, having a dark body with a crimson beak. It has long toes for walking on soft ground, and can even stand on the top of lily pads. It swims awkwardly with jerky movements, bobbing its tail up and down. The underside of this is white and flashes each time the tail jerks. This is supposed to be a useful guide for the babies to follow, so that they do not get lost among the reeds.

The larger **Coot** is even blacker, and has a white beak and face. This is how we get the saying "bald as a coot", the word "bald" meaning white, and having nothing to do with no hair on the head.

To help it swim and dive the coot has fringes to its toes, making useful paddles. Coots are now quite common on lakes and reservoirs, even inside towns, especially during the winter months.

The **Little Grebe** or **Dabchick** is an expert diver and fish hunter, which builds a floating nest like its larger cousin, the **Great Crested Grebe**, seen on larger waters. It also covers its nest when it leaves its eggs to fish.

A little bird flitting among the reeds and resembling a blue tit could be the **Willow Tit** which likes the waterside. It is the same size but instead of a blue head and a yellow underside, the head on top is a dull black and the underparts more whitish. It is probably searching for insects to feed to its young. The nest is mostly hidden in a rotting stump of a tree, such as a willow or alder.

From what you have read you can see how these water birds can live together and share food provided by ponds, whether it is plants, fish or insects. They all form part of the pond community, even though they do not actually live in the water. A hidden spot by the pondside is a good place to watch birds. Sooner or later they must come down to drink or feed.

mallard duck
with newly hatched
ducklings

flight of
tufted ducks

mallard (drake)

pochard drake and duck

dabchick

marsh tit

coot

moorhen

The Common Frog

Apart from all the animals which live their whole lives in a pond there are some that go there only to breed. One of the best known is the **Common Frog**, the only frog native to Britain. It is an **amphibian**, and like the toad and newt breeds in water. All through the winter the frogs are hidden away in a deep sleep, called **hibernation**. Some even manage to spend the winter buried in the mud at the pond bottom.

As spring approaches, they wake up and come together in breeding colonies. Each male seeks out a female, and clasps her from behind under her armpits. A female in spring is swollen up with eggs. You can tell a male by the way it croaks. A whole colony will make a dull, throbbing sound, very much like the noise of a distant motor bicycle. Also, the males have swellings on their thumbs in order to grip the females. This desire to grip a female is so strong that a male frog will even grab hold of a sluggish fish or a floating twig. I have even had one grasp my finger.

Egg-laying takes place quite rapidly. The pairs may wait for a number of days, as if waiting for some signal. Then, all together, masses of **spawn** clumps are produced. As a clump is laid by a female, it is **fertilized** in the water by the male. It is all over in a matter of hours, then the frogs leave the pond and scatter. Each egg is coated with a layer of jelly substance, and a whole clump of eggs stuck together may number up to 4,000. This jelly is not intended as food, but for protection. It also keeps out the frost. As it swells up, the mass floats to the surface, so that the eggs get the full benefit of the sun.

As each tadpole forms out of the egg, it receives food from the **yolk** cells. Depending on the weather and temperature the baby tadpole should hatch out in about twelve hours. On the next two pages you can see the stages of its growth. At first it will cling to nearby plants by means of a **mucous gland**. Later, this is where the mouth will be. Also, it has **external gills** so that it breathes in water, as fishes do. In the early stages the tadpole is a plant eater. When the mouth appears it is full of rows of tiny teeth

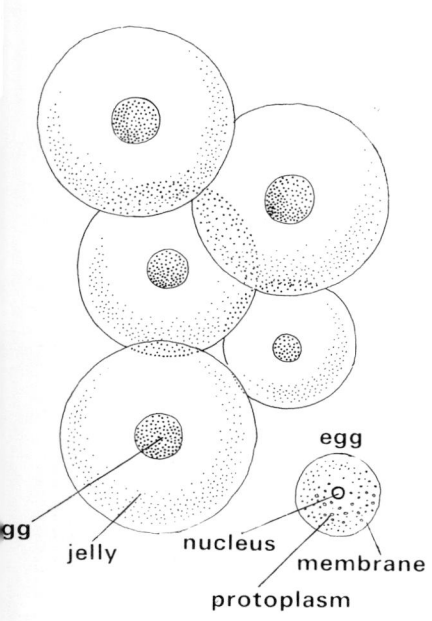

egg

gg

jelly nucleus

membrane

protoplasm

detail of frog spawn

with which it can rasp away at plants, especially the soft algae. The tail is used for swimming, for as yet there are no legs.

When legs do appear (the hind ones first, then the front pair), the gills make way for a pair of lungs. The tail begins to shorten as it is absorbed by the body for food. Also, the tadpole begins to feed on animal food by eating up dead creatures. A dead fish will attract them, and in no time is stripped of all the meat. Tadpoles will even attack a sick fish. In the aquarium they can be given small pieces of raw meat to eat.

Finally, if all goes well, a baby frog is formed in about twelve weeks, and is ready to leave the water. And so, from an egg, through a tadpole stage which is a kind of water baby, a frog is made, This is why such creatures are called **amphibians**, a Greek name meaning "two-lives". From a gill-breathing tadpole in water, a lung-breathing land frog develops.

The breeding period varies over Great Britain. In the south it takes place in early March, but in Scotland may be delayed as late as May or June. This has all to do with the late season, and because frogs are cold-blooded. Much of their energy and growth depends on the temperature.

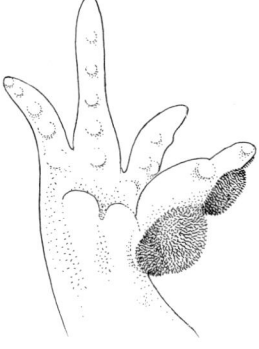

frog's clasping organ

Although we call this amphibian the Common Frog, in many parts of Britain today it is by no means common. This is due to a number of things. Many ponds are no longer in use on farmland, and have either been filled in or have dried up. Also, various weed killers and insecticides have poisoned the water and killed off the pond life. This does seem a great pity, since frogs and many pond creatures are interesting to watch and study. Also, the tadpoles produced in such great numbers make a valuable food supply in any pond, as we shall see later on.

Many animals have their legends. When the baby frogs are ready to leave the pond, they wait for some signal. Then, they all leave the water together, usually during a rain shower. If you happen to be there at the right moment you will find yourself surrounded by hundreds of tiny, leaping frogs. This has given rise to a legend that it has been "raining frogs", as if they had fallen out of the sky.

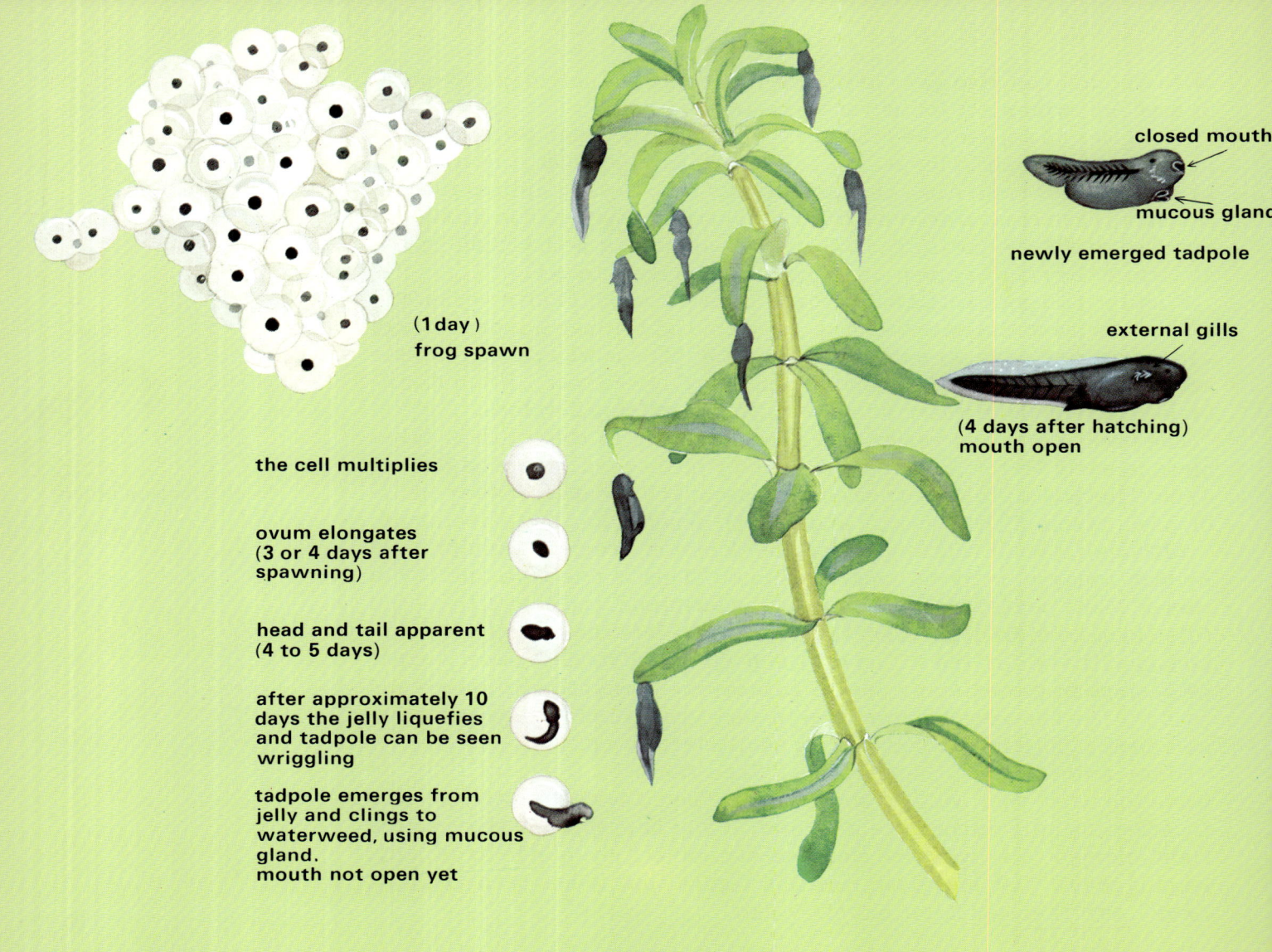

(1 day)
frog spawn

the cell multiplies

ovum elongates
(3 or 4 days after
spawning)

head and tail apparent
(4 to 5 days)

after approximately 10
days the jelly liquefies
and tadpole can be seen
wriggling

tadpole emerges from
jelly and clings to
waterweed, using mucous
gland.
mouth not open yet

closed mouth

mucous gland

newly emerged tadpole

external gills

(4 days after hatching)
mouth open

spiracle

limb bud

(3 weeks after hatching)
external gills and mucous
gland gone

forelimb
(10/11 weeks)
forelimbs develop

(10–11 weeks)
takes air at surface

(8 weeks) hind legs formed
and developed

(12–13 weeks)
mouth and eyes bigger
tail absorbed

the adult
common frog

A Food Chain

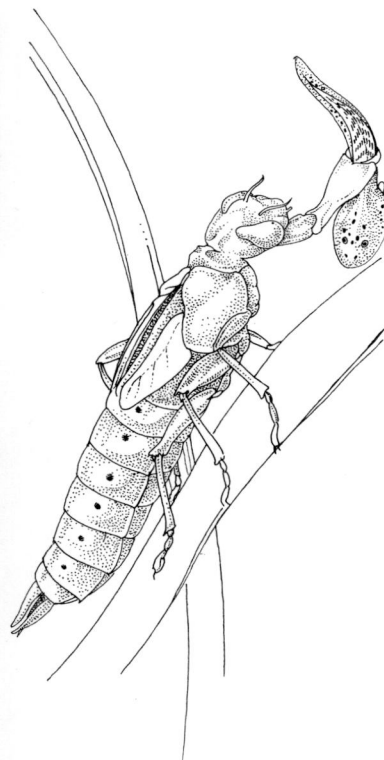

dragonfly larva
catching tadpole

One of the things that all life has in common in order to live and grow is **energy**. With non-living things that work or move, like a clock, a car or a bullet, we provide the fuel for energy. A clock is wound up by its spring, a car is given petrol, and a bullet gets its energy from the exploding cartridge.

With living things energy comes from **food**. Plants and animals get this in different ways. With a plant it comes from nature, getting say, **water**, **carbon dioxide** from the air, and **minerals** out of the ground. The last two also occur in natural water. These are called **inorganic foods**. With the help of the **chlorophyll** in its leaves a plant can build these into **organic foods**, such as starch, sugar, fat and meat.

This is what animals need as food, since they have no chlorophyll and cannot make it. It is important to know this, since it means that animals cannot exist without plants. They feed on the plants, or on other animals as we do.

In nature this feeding goes on all the time, and has to be carefully balanced out so that each kind of animal gets a fair share. By studying the feeding habits of different animals it is possible to follow through what is called a **Food Chain**. A good example can be seen in the pond community.

This food chain begins with the **microscopic plants** which multiply in millions. They drift near the surface to catch the sunlight, and make their own food with the help of chlorophyll. Most of them are one-celled algae.

This happens every spring and summer when there is plenty of sunshine and warmth, and a pond may even turn green. Then the **minute animals**, like *Amoeba* and *Paramaecium* we have already met, feed on the tiny plants. They, too, multiply.

Now it is the turn of **larger animals**, such as *Daphnia*, baby newts, young fish, and so on. These will then fall prey to **even larger animals**, such as the sticklebacks, grown newts and bigger fish. This is the time of year when most food is needed for growing youngsters.

Still the food chain goes on. A **perch** spots a **stickleback** and catches it. Even the perch may not be safe, for a **pike** is lurking in the reeds. There is a sudden rush, and the perch is captured and devoured. Maybe one day an **angler** will land the pike and take it home for supper!

You can see from all this how the numbers in a food chain get less and less as the animals get bigger. Starting with endless numbers of minute plants and animals we end up with a single fish—the pike. Being the biggest in the chain it requires most food. This balance of numbers according to the food supply is called a **Food Pyramid**.

From this we can learn something. Microscopic pond life is just as important as the big animals, for without it the pike could not live. The tiny animals at the bottom are called "key" animals. Those at the top, like the pike, are the "apex" animals.

All this feeding on one another is carefully balanced out so that each kind of animal gets a proper share.

Some times an apex animal gets too numerous in a pond or lake, and may upset the balance. I once visited a large pond which seemed empty of animal life, except for a few monster pike. They had eaten up almost everything, and were even attacking each other, being half starved. When this happens fishermen usually remove the pike so as to restore the balance.

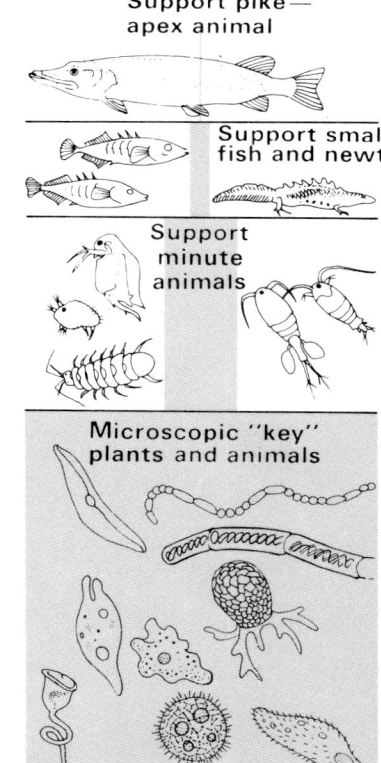

Support pike— apex animal

Support small fish and newts

Support minute animals

Microscopic "key" plants and animals

microscopic plants and animals

plants and animals
grow in sun etc.

the pikes eats
perch and sticklebacks

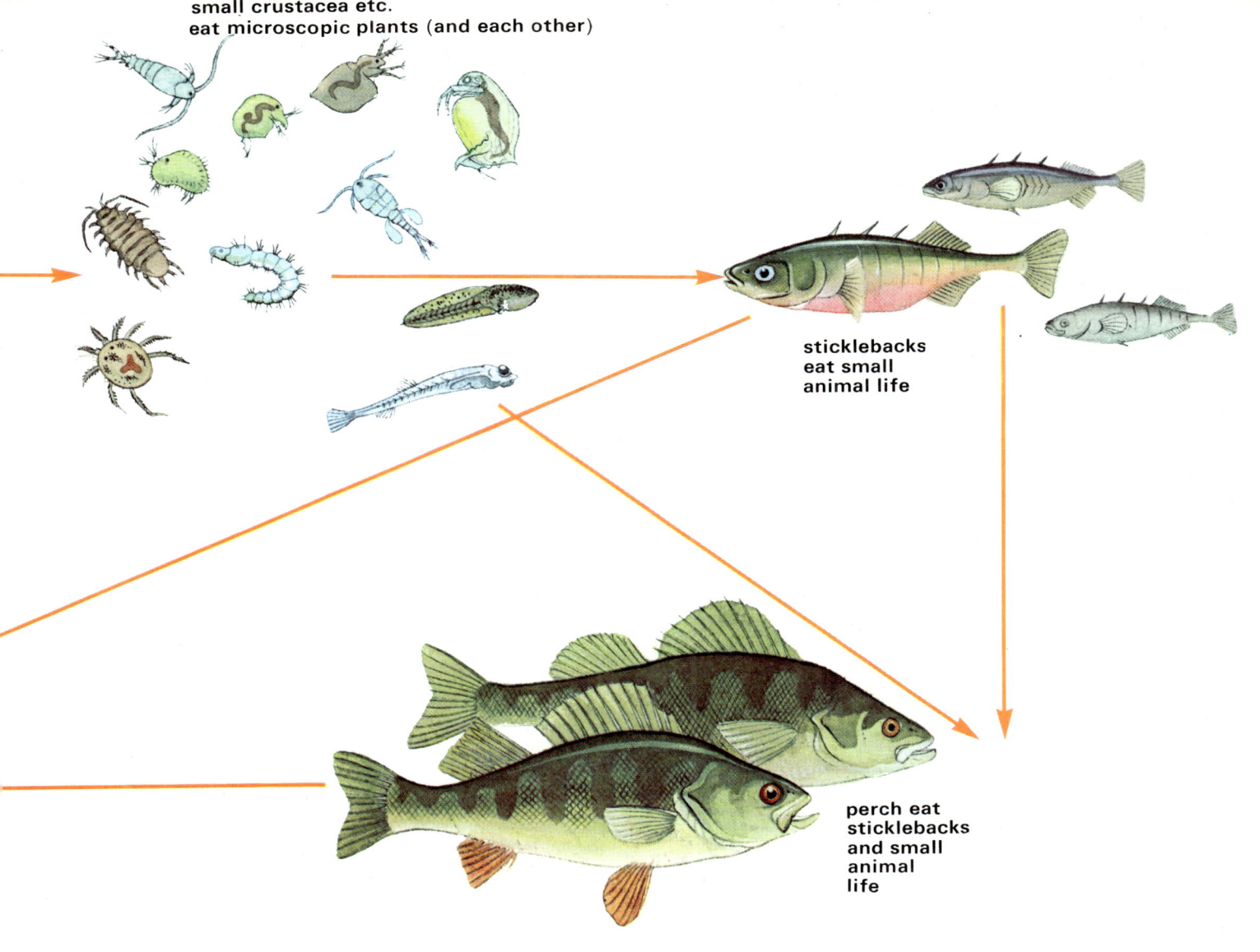

small crustacea etc.
eat microscopic plants (and each other)

sticklebacks
eat small
animal life

perch eat
sticklebacks
and small
animal
life

Summary

We have seen how ponds can contain a whole world of plants and animals. Like the rock pool on the sea-shore a pond is one of nature's own aquariums. The study of a pond community can last a lifetime, as I know from watching a pond over the past thirty years.

What interests the **ecologist**, is the way in which water life adapts itself to a world so different from ours. Obtaining **oxygen** from the water is made possible with gills, as in fish. Others, like frogs, newts, insects and some snails, come to the surface to breathe air as we do. **Swimming** in water is made easier by the use of fins, tails, webs on toes, and legs shaped like paddles. Also, the body shape is often more streamlined.

What happens when the pond freezes over? Do the inmates suffocate or freeze to death? Being cold-blooded, their body temperature drops as winter sets in and the water cools. This makes them sluggish and quiet, so that little energy is used up. In this condition, called **hibernation**, most pond creatures lie buried in the mud and debris at the pond bottom, safe and sound from enemies and freezing air, beneath a covering of ice.

Plants will have died down to their roots and storage organs. Some others form tight fitting buds which break off and rest on the bottom. These are called winter buds, and will grow into new plants next spring.

Today, alas, many of our ponds are in danger of disappearing, and are drying up or neglected, since farmers no longer need them. Others are becoming poisoned by chemicals used as weed-killers, or upset by fertilizers. Some have even been filled in and built upon. Our pond life is in danger of disappearing. This is why naturalists and conservationists are now trying to protect ponds, even building new ones, so that all this interesting wildlife shall not die out.

Having a garden pond, however small, is one way in which we can all help. Usually such a pond only contains goldfish, but a garden pond with frogs, toads, water insects, snails and so on can be just as interesting.

MARSHLAND WILDLIFE

The Marshlands

This is a book about watery places which are still found in some parts of Britain, especially in the **Eastern Counties** of England, from Norfolk down to Kent. The Norfolk Broads, the fens and meres of Lincolnshire and Cambridgeshire, the Essex marshes and the Romney marsh in Kent, are some of the larger areas which stretch for miles over the countryside and have a wild and lonely look. In wintertime the mist hangs heavy over the shallow water and reedbeds, but in fine weather there are splendid views of clouds drifting through the summer skies. In the evening there are beautiful sunsets. No wonder this is popular with artists who paint the scenery, and with visitors who like to go boating and fishing. In winter the sportsman goes out to shoot the wildfowl which gather there.

Marshland occurs where water and mud gathers in hollows or on flat ground, and is usually the work of **rivers**. Along a river bend, or where a river enters a lake, there may be a marshy place which is covered with plants which like to grow out of shallow water, and where trees like willows and alder can grow. This is the home for many water birds like ducks, waders, moorhen and grebe which nest in hidden places between the reeds and rushes.

Marshes also form along flat coasts around **river mouths**. These are called **salt marshes** if they get covered at high tide. As a river approaches the sea, it slows down, then drops the mud and silt which it has picked up on its way down.

At one time there were vast stretches of marshland down the flat eastern coast of England; these were avoided by humans because of unpleasant swampy conditions. Such land is of little use to us because we cannot build houses on it, or grow any crops. However, as the population in Britain increased, more land was needed, so many of these marshes were drained of water. This was done by building a **dyke**, or **sea-wall**, to keep out the sea. Then, behind the sea-wall, **ditches** and **canals** were dug to drain

tufted ducks

marsh harrier

away the water and dry out the land, making the ground firm for crops.

On such land, called a **salt pasture**, sheep can be reared where grass is growing. In other places root-crops like potato and sugar beet do well. Even tulips and daffodils are now grown where once the land was under the sea. There is much about this flat countryside which reminds us of Holland. The Dutch are famous for their fight against the sea and have won a lot of land by building dykes and canals.

Another reason for draining marshes in Britain was because of a sickness called the **ague** (aye-gew), meaning "shivering". People were afraid to live there and believed that this illness came from the marsh gases. We now know that it is caused by a germ carried by the mosquito which breeds in swamps; we call it **malaria**. This word actually means "bad air".

Today all this is changed and people can now live on the marshes. Many visitors go there on holiday every summer.

All this drainage to make way for farmland and homes is fine for us, but what about the marshland animals and plants which must have wet places to live in? Once common, many of them have now become rare, and some are only found in a very few places. How can we protect them, and still enjoy their company without disturbing them? One way is to have laws. Many wild birds are now **protected**: this means they must not be caught, nor may their eggs be collected. Game birds and fish have a **close season**: they must not be shot or caught during their breeding season.

Another way to protect wildlife is to set aside **nature reserves** where they will be safe. Many natural history societies and other bodies have bought up land in the marshes where the wildlife is now safe. The important thing is to preserve the habitat and leave the wildlife undisturbed.

In the following pages we shall have a look at some of these marshland animals and plants, including some of the rare ones, and see how they live and fit into their watery surroundings.

Marshland Plants

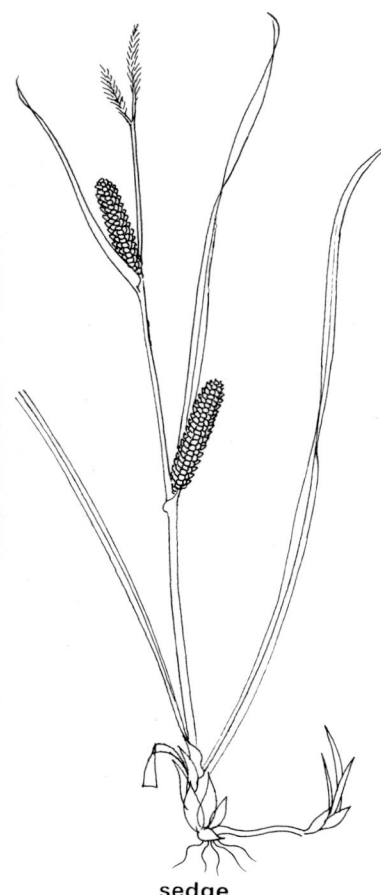

sedge

One of the commonest plants growing on the marshes is the **Reed**. This is our tallest grass, growing up to eight feet tall, and has an attractive, plume-like head of tiny flowers. It grows at the waterside, mostly standing in shallow water, and stretches for miles, especially in the Broads. When the wind blows, ripples of movement pass through the reed beds, just like the waving corn in the wheat field.

The reed beds make ideal cover for many kinds of water birds. Here they can nest and hide in safety.

Cutting the reeds in wintertime for making **thatch** is one of Britain's oldest crafts, and many a marshland cottage is covered with reeds.

Another plant which was once cut and used during the Middle Ages is the **Sweet Flag**. If you crush the leaves, it gives off a pleasant scent. In days when carpets were scarce, layers of sweet flag were spread over the stone floors of castles. When people walked on them and crushed the flags, the rooms were kept fresh.

The sweet flag grows along the waterside, mostly in southern England. It has tall, thin leaves, rather like those of the **Water Iris**, and a round stem bearing a tight bunch of tiny, greenish flowers.

Many kinds of water plant, called **Sedges**, grow in wet places. They look grass-like, but you can tell the difference by the stem. In a grass this is rounded. In a sedge it is triangular. Also, the clusters of flowers usually grow in separate bunches, the male on top and the female below.

One of our most beautiful waterside plants is the **Flowering Rush**. The small, rose-pink flowers grow on stalks which spread out from the main stem like the ribs of an open umbrella. Flowers appear in August and you may see a patch growing among the reeds and rushes.

Growing on the mud and in shallow water is a beautiful plant called the **Bogbean**. It creeps along as it grows, sending up large, three-lobed leaves looking somewhat like large clover leaves. Between these are stalks bearing pretty flowers. Each has five petals, pink on the outside, and

76

fringed with hairs giving it a fluffy look.

One kind of waterside plant you should look for is the **Horsetail**. There are a number of kinds, growing to about three feet tall, each plant consisting of a stem which has rings of spiky leaves giving the plant a brush-like appearance. These plants have no flowers. Instead, a club-shaped growth appears at the tip, from which minute **spores** are set free when it ripens.

These primitive plants are survivors of the ancient **Carboniferous Period** when there were giant horsetails as tall as trees. These have long since disappeared and their remains turned into coal buried deep in the earth's crust.

It is always exciting to find a wild **Orchid**. Those found in Britain are rather small, but just as beautiful as tropical orchids. One of them, called the **Marsh Orchid**, is fairly common and grows in damp meadows and marshy places. The flowers vary from pale pink to a deep purple. Orchids can only grow well if a certain kind of fungus grows inside their roots. This is why orchids usually die if we uproot them and put them into the wrong soil. In any case some are now far too rare to take away and should be left alone.

Various plants can grow in the open water of a marsh. In most places you will find the water surface covered with flat, oval leaves of a greenish-brown colour. This could be one of the **Pondweeds**. The roots are in the mud at the bottom, and every summer long stems grow to the surface so that the leaves can float. Here and there a flower stalk rises up, covered with many small, dull-coloured flowers. A patch of pondweed is a good hiding place for fish. Also, this is where the fish can lay their eggs.

You will have noticed that many of these marshland plants stand in water, especially the reeds and rushes. They grow tall and thin and are closely packed together. This is because of the rich mud and plentiful water where plants grow well. Hardly a square foot is wasted. Also, the long leaves and steams bend easily when the wind blows. If they were stiff, they might snap off.

pondweeds

soft rush

flowering rush

marsh orchid

water
forget-me-not

reeds

bogbean

broadleaved
pondweed

horsetail

Marshland Mammals

fore right

hind right

footprints of otter

Animals which have hair on, like ourselves, are called **mammals**. They feed their young on milk. Some of them live in marshy places. To live successfully they need to be able to swim, and this is why they are usually more streamlined in shape and have webbed feet. The fur is short and thick to keep out the water and to hold in the body warmth, even when it is icy cold. Some mammals have tails which they can use as rudders for steering. The eyes and nostrils are placed more on top of the head, so that they can breathe and see above the water, yet remain mostly hidden from enemies.

The **Otter** is a good example. This is one of our most graceful and charming animals. Today, alas, it is getting very rare and this is not entirely due to the otter hunters. A far more serious danger is the poisons which get into water and kill off the fish and other water creatures. As a result, the otter has left these polluted places and gone to cleaner and wilder areas away from man to search for food.

Being a shy and lonely animal which wanders a lot, the otter is not easy to spot, but with luck you may hear one whistling on a quiet marsh, even on a reservoir where there are fish. Next day it may be miles away.

The best way to search for otters is to look for the five-toed footprint, called a **seal**. Huntsman call the tail a **rudder**. The male otter is a **dog**, the female a **bitch**. The place where an otter rests is its **hover**, and the home where the cubs are born a **holt**.

It is delightful to watch otters at play. They swim and dive in the water, often playing with a stick or stone, and in winter will slide down a bank of snow or along the ice.

Otter cubs may be born any time of the year. The mother teaches them how to swim. At first they are afraid and may even have to be picked up and dropped in for their first lesson. The careful mother then carries them on her back if they get into difficulty.

What you can more easily see today is another water mammal, almost as big, called a **Coypu**. This comes from South America, and is bred for its fur, called **nutria**. A number escaped from the fur farms and are living wild in the Norfolk marshes. The coypu tunnels into banks and can do some damage by causing flooding. Also, it may harm some of the crops by digging up bulbs and potatoes. Coypus are now being trapped and shot to keep down their numbers.

If you should see one, it will look like a huge rat, but is really a cousin of the porcupine, but without quills. At night on the Broads you may hear a strange moaning sound. This is the call of the coypu. The babies are delightful little creatures and sometimes kept as pets. Almost from the moment they are born, these babies can swim. They can also feed from the mother in the water without choking. This is because her nipples are placed along the sides of the body. The coypu is a vegetarian and feeds mostly on the water plants.

Quite different, and only a midget in size, is the tiny **Water Shrew**. It is about four inches long. Its fur is a slaty black and the underside white. Shrews, unlike mice, are active hunters and always seem to be twitching their long, whiskered noses in search of food. They may dive into the water and look like a moving ball of quicksilver. This is because of the air bubbles caught in the fur. Under water the air shines like silver.

Small creatures, including little fish, as well as earthworms, are the food of the water shrew. Shrews have tremendous appetites as I discovered when I kept one for a while in an aquarium. It needed feeding every hour.

The **Water Vole** is a pleasant mammal, belonging to the rodent family. It is sometimes called a water rat, which is wrong. Rats have big ears, pointed snouts and long tails. Voles have small ears, blunt faces and short tails. Also, the water vole is usually quite harmless and feeds mainly on water plants. Look for the rushes and other waterside plants which have been bitten off. The small footprints can be found in the mud at the waterside.

head of water vole

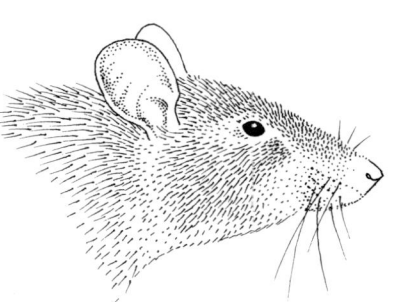

head of rat

coypu
and young

water
shrew

otter

water vole

Marshland Birds

The lonely marshlands and mud-flats of Britain are the gathering places of flocks of **Geese**, **Ducks** and **Waders** who come south every autumn to spend the winter there. During the summer they have been up in the Arctic to breed and rear their young. Then they **migrate** south; sometimes you can see them fly over in **formation**, making arrows in the sky.

At one time large numbers of these wildfowl were shot, and some of the species began to decrease alarmingly. Today an attempt is being made both by wildfowlers and naturalists to give them protection. Areas of marshland have been set aside as **sanctuaries** where no shooting is allowed.

In other places there are **nature reserves** giving total protection. At one such sanctuary, called Minsmere, is one of our rarest birds, the little **Bearded Tit.** The cock bird has a stripe of black feathers down each side of its cheeks looking somewhat like a moustache. It nests close to the ground in the undergrowth and is a clever little acrobat as it slips through the reed stems searching for insects and seeds.

In the Norfolk Broads you may hear a strange noise coming from the reed beds, a kind of booming "whoomp". This is the cry of another shy and rare bird, the **Bittern.** It looks like a small heron with a short neck. Its sharp beak is used for spearing frogs, fish and other water creatures and it has feet with long toes for standing on the soft mud. Its brown feathers, streaked with black, are a perfect match for the reed stems. When alarmed, it sits tight and sticks its head and beak straight upwards. In this odd position it is well camouflaged.

Another sight over the open marshes is an owl which flies by day. This is the **Short-eared Owl.** It flaps and glides low over the ground in search of small animals such as the field vole. It also hunts rabbits. This owl nests on the ground, sometimes using an old rabbit burrow.

Another marshland hunter is the **Marsh Harrier**, a bird-of-prey which comes over every year as a summer visitor. It also hunts small animals and will fly steadily backwards and forwards over the marshes and fens,

great crested
grebes courting

low over the ground, until it spots something. Then it drops onto its prey. Harriers have rather small heads, slender bodies, pointed wings and long tails.

The marsh harrier builds a large nest on the ground among the reeds, and people who are fond of birds will put up notices, or even stand on guard to keep away strangers, so that the chicks may be reared in safety.

A far more common sight on the marshes is one of the waders, called a **Redshank**. It has a long, red beak and legs which it uses for paddling in the shallow water and probing in the mud for food. You can hear its musical call, a piping "teu-hu-hu" echoing over the marsh. It is also common on moorlands where it feeds in the bogs. The redshank nests on the ground among the clumps of grass.

My favourite marsh bird is the handsome **Great Crested Grebe**. It is an expert fisherman with a streamlined body, sharp beak and feet with webbed toes. It dives under the water for its food.

When two grebes pair off they will court one another by swimming round in circles, rubbing necks together and "kissing" with their beaks. The male will offer his mate bits of water plant; this is a kind of invitation to build a nest. This is fixed to some reed stems out on the water and actually floats. The parents take turns in sitting on the eggs and always cover them up when they leave to go fishing.

At one time this lovely bird was hunted for the feathers which grow round its neck. Today it is protected. Many grebes are now found on reservoirs where they can fish and nest in peace, even in built-up areas. I have even seen a pair on a reservoir in the heart of London.

Another marsh dweller is a little summer visitor, the **Reed Warbler**. It is a brownish colour and has a thin, pointed beak for catching insects. It has a pretty, warbling song which can sometimes be heard at night. This warbler builds a nest by twisting grass and other plant material around some reed stems over the water. This is a safe place for the young.

reed warbler on nest

black headed gull

short eared owl

marsh harrier

great crested grebe

redshanks

geese

reed warbler

bitterns

bearded tit

The Mute Swan

There is one kind of water bird we all know – the **Mute Swan**. It is a very tame bird and turns up on most ponds, rivers and marshes, even along the seashore. We throw bread to it, and can sometimes meet a whole family out for a swim.

This swan should not be confused with the truly wild swans which fly up north every spring to breed in the Arctic, then return to us for the winter to rest on the lonely marshes and mud-flats. There are two kinds which visit Britain: the **Bewick** and **Whooper Swans**. If you ever see one of these, notice that the neck is held up stiffly. The mute swan carries its neck in a graceful S-curve. Also, it has a black swelling on top of its beak, called a **berry**.

The tame swan gets its name because it is rather silent, or mute, apart from making a few hisses and snorts. Also, its wings make a creaking sound when it flies. Its main home is along the shores of the old Zuyder Zee in Holland.

The male, called a **cob**, has a large berry on its beak, and gets very annoyed if another cob invades its territory. His wife, called a **pen**, has a smaller berry. In the spring she gets busy building a large nest made of sticks and plant material. Her babies, fluffy little grey chicks, are called cygnets. They hatch out in about May. By mid-summer they are nearly as big as their mother, but a brownish colour. Only in the second year do they turn white.

The swan is a good example of a water bird which is adapted for life on water. Although it can weigh as much as 15 pounds, it floats quite easily. Its body is boat-shaped and is pushed along with strong, webbed feet. The long neck is useful for pushing under the water to probe about in the mud, or to reach for water plants on which it normally feeds. Although we like to feed it on bread, a swan's real food is plant material, even seaweeds along the seashore. Around the edge of its beak is a kind of comb-like fringe which acts as a strainer. The water can pass through it when

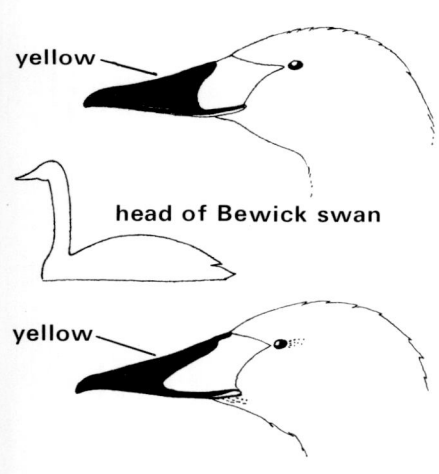

yellow

head of Bewick swan

yellow

head of whooper swan

orange

head of mute swan

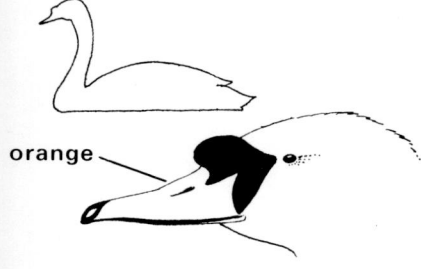

it squeezes its food. It will do the same thing with a crust of bread.

Many centuries ago one of our kings admired this beautiful bird so much that he chose it as his own. Ever since it has been called the royal swan. From time to time down the years our kings and queens would give permission for various people to keep their own swans as a reward for helping the country in some way.

Each collection of swans was called a **herd** and, to recognise his own swans, each owner would mark the beaks by cutting little **notches** on them. Marking was done to stop poaching, because years ago swans were eaten. If you were caught stealing one you could go to prison.

Today, the marking of swans has nearly died out, except along the river Thames. Many of the swans living there belong to the Crown. These are called the **Queen's birds**. Others belong to the two old City of London companies, the **Dyers' company** and the **Vintners' company**.

Every July when the swans are on the river with their grown cygnets an old ceremony takes place. Men in long rowing boats, dressed in bright costumes, go searching for swans in order to mark their beaks. This is called **Swan-upping**. If somebody spots a family, he shouts out "Swan up".

Then the boats move in to trap the swans against the bankside. Now comes the difficult part, how to catch a grown swan. This can be dangerous and is the job only for a grown man. The beat of a swan's wing is powerful and could break a leg or arm.

When the men have found out who owns the parents they then mark the cygnets according to their owners. In this way, for hundreds of years, swans have been marked on the Thames.

It is no wonder that this beautiful and graceful bird is protected and is a favourite with poets and artists. There are also many stories and legends about swans. One of them, quite untrue, is that a swan sings just before it dies; this is called its **swan-song**.

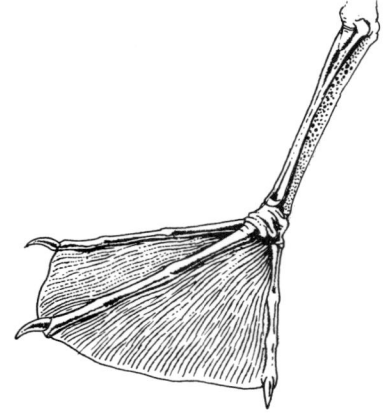

swan's webbed foot

nest of
mute swan

mute swan
and young cygnets

Bewick's swan

mute swan threatening

Frogs in the Marshes

Marshes have always been favourite places for frogs. This is where they can hide from their many enemies. More important, it is where they can breed. Frogs, like toads and newts, are **amphibians** with a baby stage, called a **tadpole**. This has gills to start with and breathes like a fish. This means that it must grow up in water.

All through the winter the frogs are hidden away in the mud, fast asleep. Some of them can even hibernate at the bottom of the marsh. When spring arrives, they wake up and seek their mates. This is when you can hear them croaking, if you move quietly towards the waterside.

In some countries, especially in the tropics, the noise can be deafening. As the rains begin and the ponds and marshes fill up, the frogs begin their nightly chorus, an amazing mixture of croaks, trills and whistles. You have to get used to all this noise and it keeps some people awake.

In Britain this is not much of a problem, since the only one, the **Common Frog**, only makes a rather dull croaking sound. There are two others, however, which can be quite noisy during the summer. Both have been introduced from Europe.

One of these is the **Edible Frog,** a beautiful creature coloured bright green or bronze, which has a pale stripe down its back. It is very aquatic, and anyone visiting Holland, Belgium, France, Germany or Italy, must have heard it. This frog got its name from a custom in France where it is caught and eaten. Usually the hind legs are cooked, tasting like chicken.

From May until mid-summer the edible frogs are gathered in their thousands along the canals and in the lakes and marshes where they spawn. The males blow up the loose skin at both corners of their mouths into little balloons. These act as sound boxes, so that a whole colony in full cry sounds quite loud.

On a number of occasions these frogs have been brought over and set free in the Norfolk Broads and the Cambridgeshire fens. The earliest introduction was in 1837. This was an ideal home for them and they

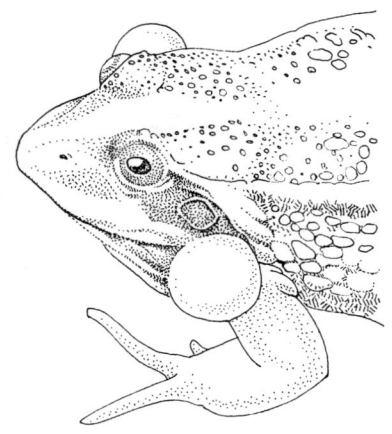
head of marsh frog

92

multiplied in great numbers. At night their calls were so loud, that people named them **Cambridgeshire Nightingales**.

Then something went wrong. A little before World War II they began to die off and today there are almost none left. Nobody knows why. It could have been due to pollution of the water, which is now upsetting so many water creatures, or maybe the weather in Britain is not quite right for them. Perhaps their enemies, such as grebes, herons and otters, were too much for them.

In 1934 the second frog arrived in this country – the **Marsh Frog**. It looks like an edible frog but is much bigger and stronger. In that year twelve of these frogs, which came from Hungary, were set free in a pond in the middle of the Romney marsh, in Kent. This was done to try and keep down the mosquitoes on which they feed. The Romney marsh is flat countryside, once under the sea, and now protected by dykes and canals as they do in Holland. It consists mostly of small fields surrounded by water ditches. These criss-cross the marsh for miles and were just right for the frogs to live in. They soon escaped from the pond and are now all over the marshland.

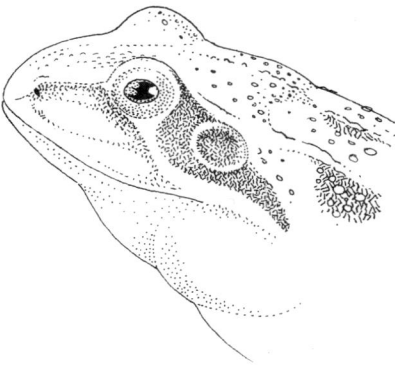

In summer you can see them sitting on the banks, but being very shy they quickly dive in if you disturb them. Towards evening, and all night long in warm weather they croak loudly, and the people on the marshes call them **Laughing Frogs**.

Although still quite common, there are signs that the Marsh Frog is dying off in some places. Some of the ditches are being covered in to make bigger fields, because some farmers are now growing crops, also many ditches are getting choked with water weeds so there is little room to move. The Romney marsh has always been famous for rearing sheep, for which these small fields with water ditches were ideal. Now the sheep are disappearing. If all the ditches should ever disappear, then perhaps the cry of the Laughing Frog will no longer be heard over the marshland.

head of common frog

edible frog

marsh frog

common frog

Fishes

In the open marshes live a number of freshwater fishes which prefer still waters. The fisherman who tries to catch them has to be a bit of a naturalist and understand their habits – how they live and what they feed on.

For example, the **Common Carp** is a slow-moving fish which feeds mainly on plant material and on what it can find in the mud at the bottom. It has feelers, or **barbels**, at the corner of its mouth and these are very sensitive. It grubs about for food on the bottom, but sometimes on warm summer evenings will rise to the surface to pick up whatever has fallen in. You can hear a sucking noise as it "blows bubbles" among the reeds. When the sun is out, it will bask at the surface and even refuse to take the fisherman's bait. The famous fisherman Izaak Walton called it a "fox", meaning that it is clever and difficult to catch.

During winter the carp will retire to deeper water and sleep through the cold weather buried in the mud. A carp can be frozen in the ice, yet it will survive. It can be kept alive for hours, wrapped in a wet cloth.

Sometimes called the **Old English Carp** this fish originally came from China, and was introduced by the monks who kept them in fish-ponds so that they could be eaten on certain days when meat was not allowed. Carp can lay hundreds of thousands of tiny eggs and grow up to a large size, weighing as much as 20 pounds or more.

The **Tench** is another bottom dweller and lives best in weedy and muddy parts of the marsh where another fish might feel uncomfortable. It can be recognised by its deep, olive-brown colour, rounded fins, and a slime-covered skin which has very tiny scales. At one time it was said that this slime purified the water and helped to keep other fish healthy. This is why it is sometimes called the **Doctor Fish**.

Also found in still water is the portly-shaped **Bream**. It has a small head; from above it looks very thin, but from the side has a deep and rounded shape. Bream generally live in shoals and wander about a good deal, sometimes travelling for miles up and down the canals and lakes in the

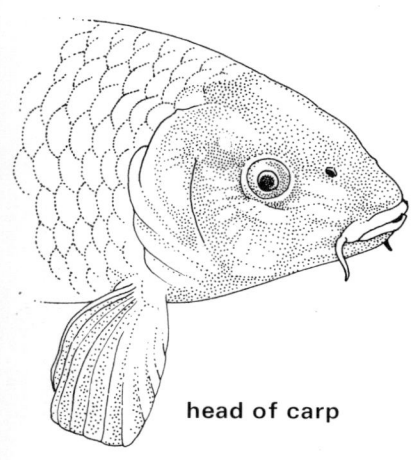

head of carp

Broads. Like the carp the bream grubs about in mud in search of worms and various water insects. A good sized bream can weigh up to 12 pounds.

Quite different in appearance and habits is the **Rudd**. It has a dark blue-brown colour tinged with gold, and the fins and tail are a deep red. Its body is more streamlined for cruising about the canals and marshes. Like the bream it is commonest in East Anglia. Among the weeds and reedbeds it searches for water insects and shrimps; it will readily come to the surface if you throw out a piece of bread. Some fisherman call the rudd the **Red-eye** because of the colour of its eyes. A good specimen weighs between 2–3 pounds.

All these fish are rather slow-moving vegetarians, but, as in all groups of animals, there are hunting fish as well. One of the largest and fiercest of these is the **Pike**. It has a long, torpedo-shaped body with a flattened head, and a very large mouth full of sharp teeth. There are even teeth on its tongue. The back or dorsal fin lies well back, near the tail.

head of pike

The pike does not chase after its prey, but waits patiently among the reeds until a smaller fish passes by. Then it makes a sudden rush to catch it. For this kind of hunting it is well camouflaged. The body colour is a pale greenish-grey, marked with dark upright stripes which blend perfectly with the water and reed stems. Fishermen will catch a pike by using an artificial model of a fish, or a bright metal spoon, which is covered in hooks. This is wound in so that the imitation fish twists and turns in the water, much like a real fish. This may tempt the hidden pike.

Baby water fowl such as ducklings are sometimes caught from below and dragged under. There are even cases of people getting their fingers grabbed if they trail them in the water from a boat. No wonder Izaak Walton called this fish a "river wolf". Monsters of up to 30 pounds have been caught in Britain. A young pike is called a **Jack**, and a baby a **Pickerel**. Pike sometimes turn up in new water where they have been introduced by birds. The sticky eggs are carried on their legs.

pike

carp

tench

rudd

bream

The Swallowtail Butterfly

Many people who visit the Norfolk Broads do not realize that they are in the home of a rare insect, a beautiful butterfly called the **Swallowtail**. It is brightly coloured in black and yellow, and gets its name from the "tail" on each wing.

With luck you may see one in summer flying over the reeds. In May or June the female searches for somewhere to lay her eggs. She is looking for a plant on which the **caterpillars** feed – the **Milk Parsley**.

Eggs are laid singly on this and are difficult to find. A better place to look is in a garden or field where carrots are growing. The female will also lay eggs on this.

The baby caterpillar is at first rather dull, looking just like a bird dropping. This helps to camouflage it from enemies. Its first meal is the egg-shell. Then it starts to eat ravenously on the milk parsley leaves, changing its skin from time to time.

A grown caterpillar is very handsome. It is brightly coloured in green, with circles of black rings down the body dotted with orange spots.

It is fascinating to watch the change into a **chrysalis**. First, the caterpillar makes a pad of silk on a reed stem and grips it tightly with its hind legs. Next, it spins a silken girdle round its body which is also fixed to the stem so that it does not fall off. It then skins for the last time and turns into the chrysalis. All through the winter the chrysalis remains in its shell. The marshmen who cut the reeds for thatching the cottage roofs sometimes find these **chrysalids** (the plural of **chrysalis**) in wintertime.

Next year, as the weather warms up in May, a beautiful butterfly emerges. This is the time when you may see a male (the smaller butterfly) chasing a female. When they have mated and separated, the female starts laying her eggs, and the process begins all over again.

Sometimes a chrysalis fails to change into a butterfly. This could be due to another insect, called an **Ichneumon Fly**. With its long egg-tube it pierces a caterpillar and lays its eggs inside. The grub which hatches

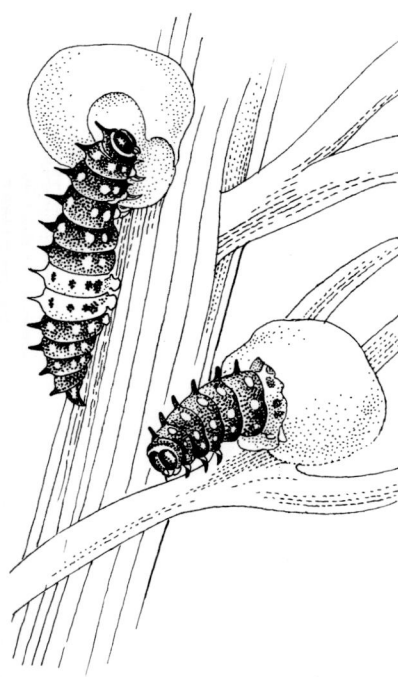

caterpillar emerging from egg

then feeds on the live caterpillar; yet the caterpillar still manages to turn into a chrysalis. Even so this ends up as an empty shell with a hole through which the new ichneumon fly has emerged. You may be able to find such an empty chrysalis still attached to a reed stem.

As long as there are marshy places where the milk parsley grows the swallowtail will stay with us. Let us hope that this is always so.

One curious thing about this butterfly is that on the Continent it lives in woods, whereas over here it belongs to the marshes. What seems to have happened is that the British butterflies were cut off from those in Europe. During the Ice Age Britain was connected with France, but when the ice melted and the sea rose, she became an island. This is how the swallowtail, and indeed many other animals and plants, were separated into two groups, those on the Continent, and those over here. For some reason we do not know why the British colony settled in the marshes instead of the woods.

Not so long ago there were swallowtails living in marshy places along the river Thames, but these have now disappeared because of drainage. There are now houses and streets where the swallowtail used to fly.

This ability to live in different surroundings, or habitats, is quite common among some animals and plants, although it is a slow business. We humans with our brains and skill manage this best of all and can live in such different surroundings as forests, deserts, mountains, marshes, even on the Antarctic. One day we may even be living on the moon.

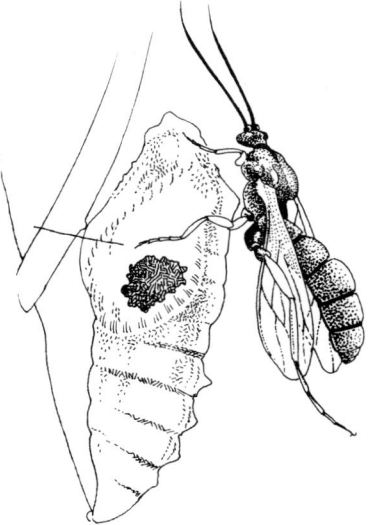

ichneumon fly
emerging from chrysalis
of swallowtail

1
the
imago

3
young
caterpillar

4
mature
caterpillar

5
about to
turn into a
chrysalis

2
eggs

6
shedding
skin

7
the chrysalis

8
emerging
from the
chrysalis

9
drying
the wings

10
the imago

Summary

We have seen some of the wild animals and plants which make their home in the marshes. To a naturalist these are precious parts of Britain which need to be preserved and kept clean. There are so few of them left. Marsh life changes with the seasons.

All **winter** the marsh lies still and silent under the cold sky, sometimes beneath a blanket of snow and ice. Yet there is still life there. The fish lie torpid in the deeper water, except maybe for the hunting pike and winter fisherman trying to catch it. Frogs are buried in the mud, fast asleep. The waterfowl are huddled together in patches of water which has not yet frozen. If you are lucky, you may find a toboggan slide in the snow where the otters have been playing. Most of the signs of life are out on the mudflats and salt marshes where the geese settle to feed and sleep.

As **spring** arrives, the geese and duck will fly north to spend the summer rearing their young in the Arctic. One or two spring flowers, like the marsh marigold and primrose, will brighten up the dull landscape. Reddish catkins dangle from the branches of the alder tree and fluffy seeds appear on the willow. By May the marsh frogs will be stirring in the Romney marsh. Both fishes and frogs are now spawning, and the heron and bittern are kept busy at the waterside trying to catch them for their youngsters.

Summer is a busy time for insects. You can see dragonflies darting about, various kinds of beetles rising to the surface and, if you are lucky you may spot a rare **Swallowtail Butterfly** fluttering among the reeds. The Swan's brood is now fully grown and the water shrew has had a family.

By autumn most of this will have died down. Frogs and fish disappear, the swallowtail is in the chrysalis stage, and the ducks have returned from the north, but the holiday visitors have gone.

Next year the **cycle of life** will start all over again. However, if we continue to poison and drain away the water, all that we have read here may one day disappear.

RIVER LIFE

The River

High up in the mountains a river is born. **Rain** falling on the high places runs downhill and forms tiny trickles which wash into the cracks, or settle in small mountain pools between the stones and rocks. Some of this rainwater sinks into the ground, but a good deal runs over the surface, gradually forming into little channels. It is a beginning of a river which will finally end up in the sea or some lake.

As each tiny **stream** moves downhill, it is joined by others so that a baby river is formed.

As we move downstream larger and larger **sidestreams,** called **tributaries,** join up so that the young river increases in size. Up in the hills such a river seems to be full of life. This is because of the mountain slope down which it runs. In its youth, it is lively and musical, bubbling around the rocks, splashing over rocks in little waterfalls, and even pushing aside stones which get in the way. It is always in a hurry.

At last the young river reaches the foothills and comes out into the flatter, open countryside. The slope is far less, so it slows down. It is more grown-up and not in so much of a hurry to reach the sea. Instead of running along a straight course, it winds over a wide plain in curves across the lowland. The river water is deeper and the valley wider with gentler slopes. This called the **flood plain** and after heavy rain it may get covered in water. In this way mud gets carried over the land and makes it useful for farming. If you look at a map of Britain you can see the bends in the larger rivers, such as the **Thames.**

Still water feels soft and gentle to the touch, but when it moves fast it can become very powerful. Rushing water during a flood or storm can cause great damage. Along its course the river is continually washing away the earth and wearing down the rocks. Pieces of stone which fall into the river bed are worn smooth into pebbles.

When heavy rain causes a river to rise, the water turns cloudy. This is called a **spate**. The river is carrying along particles of mud and tiny stones, even larger ones at times. All these are being worn away from the mountainside as the river cuts its way into the ground. Lower down, near the river mouth, the river slows as it meets the sea. In some rivers the rising tide even turns the water back in the opposite direction. A wave of water, called a **bore**, travels upstream.

At the river mouth, or estuary, much of the mud or sand material is dropped to form **mudbanks** and **sandbanks**, making new land even in the sea. The river may even split up to form a **delta**.

In time a river can slowly wear away whole mountains, and the very sand we play with on the beach could have come from a mountain top a long way inland.

Here and there a river is born as a **spring**. This is where rainwater sinks into the mountain or hillside, and then finds its way out lower down. This usually happens where a soft rock like chalk or sand lies on a hard rock. The water seeps through and then travels along the top of the hard rock until it comes into the open as the beginning of a river.

A journey along a river, from its birthplace to its mouth, will show how much it changes. Its size, depth, speed and temperature alter along its course. It deepens and darkens with mud after storms, and may almost dry up during a drought. All this affects the plant and animal life which has to adapt itself to these different conditions. Some of the river life is always there, and other life comes to feed or breed in the river. Others use the waterway for travelling, like the eel and salmon. We shall now look at some of this river life, to see how it fits into running water.

The Young River

Up in the hills and mountains where a river is still young and small, the water is pure and shallow, and rich in **oxygen**. Yet it seems almost empty of life. This is far from being so, and is due to the fast running water. As with the animals on the tidal sea-shore, life in a mountain stream must cling onto something, or else it would be washed away.

Pick up any stone in such a stream, and you will almost certainly find some tiny water creature clinging to it. This could be a small **Water Snail** or an insect grub like the larva of the **Caddis Fly** which builds around itself a house of tiny stones or twigs. Some of these animals even live on top of the stones, in a film of water where the water splashes over them.

Water in a mountain stream can feel very cold, even at mid-summer. You will soon find this out if you paddle in one of the pools. The tiny water creatures can stand this cold and are even active in winter. It is said that some of them were alive in Britain during the Ice Age, and still exist in mountain streams.

In the water itself are few plants, except for **Mosses** and **Liverworts** growing on the wet stones and rocks. **Rushes** and **Willows** grow along the bankside. In boggy places there should be plenty of **Bog-moss**, which gives us a useful warning not to walk there. **Heather** is quite common if the soil is acid, and in some places you may be lucky in finding a patch of the handsome **Royal Fern**. Its fruits grow in clusters on separate stalks. The **Hart's-tongue Fern** has fronds shaped like a tongue, and is easy to recognise.

Cotton-grass is an interesting plant which grows seeds that ripen into a white cluster, looking like a tuft of cotton-wool. A few small-sized fish live in mountain streams, but are usually hidden. Gently lift up a stone and you may spot one. The **Loach** is a slender little fish, about 12 cm long. It has whiskers or barbels around its mouth for feeling among the stones in search of food, such as small worms and crustaceans.

caddis fly case

Another fish with a large head could be a **Bullhead** or **Miller's-thumb**. It got this second name because it is supposed to resemble the swollen thumb of a miller. Years ago millers used to squeeze the dough with their hands. The Bullhead will prepare a simple nest by clearing a space among the stones to lay and guard its eggs.

The pride of any hill stream is the **Brown Trout**, a beautiful, speckled river fish. To catch it, the fly fisherman fixes an artificial fly to a hook on the end of a line, and flicks it over the water, hoping that the trout will rise and catch it. When stationary on the stream bed, a trout is well camouflaged against the stones. It feeds on the various water creatures which fall in. One favourite is the **Mayfly**. Great swarms hatch out in spring and only live a short while; as they die, they fall into the water.

Do not be surprised if you come across an animal looking like a small lobster. This is the **Crayfish** which hides under stones and scavenges for anything it can find, or grabs at something with its pincers. The female, called a **hen**, carries her eggs, called **berries**, until they hatch. The babies then cling to their mother for a while, until they are strong enough to fend for themselves.

There are some birds which make their home in the hill stream. The **Dipper** or **Water Ousel** is dark-coloured with a white breast; it is about the size of a thrush, but built more like a robin. Standing on a stone, it is constantly bobbing up and down. This lively bird can dive under water and walk along the river bed in search of food. Its nest is in the river bank, often behind a waterfall.

It is with us all the year round, but the **Ring Ousel** is a summer visitor. It looks like a blackbird with a white "collar" around its neck. It nests among the rocks or heather, usually near water.

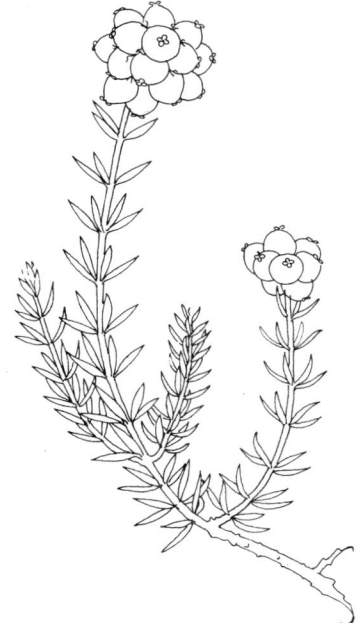

cross-leaved heather

rush

willow

royal fern

dipper

brown trout

moss

crayfish

cotton grass

mayflies

willow

hart's tongue fern

ring ousel

loach

bullhead

The Lowland Reach

perch catching fish

As the river leaves the hills and approaches the sea, its size and character changes. Broader and deeper, it moves more slowly in twists and curves. Along its banks are plenty of bushes and trees giving cover and nest sites for the birds. Trees that enjoy damp soil are most common, such as the Willows and Alder.

Life along the lowland part of the river seems to move at a slower pace. On warm days the cattle in the meadows come down to drink and cool off in the water, or stand in the shade of the trees. This is where you and I might have our picnic on a warm afternoon. Here and there a fisherman sits quietly on the bank, his rod poking through a gap in the reeds.

In the lower part of the river live a number of fish. Unlike those which live in the still water of ponds and marshes, these river fish are usually more active, and swim about in **shoals**. One such shoal fish is the **Roach**, a favourite with the angler. Looking much like the **Rudd** of quieter waters, it can be distinguished by its back fin which lies further forward. A really good specimen may weigh up to 2 pounds (approx. 1 kilo). It feeds on water plants and small animal life.

The more lively **Dace** has a silvery body, and will often come to the surface after insects which have fallen in. Both these fishes have smooth, streamlined bodies to swim against the current, and to avoid enemies such as the **Heron**.

Hidden among the reeds may be a **Perch**. He is a hunter, like the **Pike**, so is well camouflaged. Dark bands on his body match up with the reed stems. Unlike most fish the perch has a double fin on its back. When a smaller fish passes by, it will dash out to capture it. The fisherman will bait his hook with a worm to catch perch.

Roach, dace and perch usually keep to the deeper parts of the river. You will notice along the river bends how the water is much deeper on the outer curve, but quite shallow on the inner one. This is where gravel and sand collects, and in this shallower water the smaller river fish can be seen, such as the lively little **Minnow**.

About 8–10 cm long, it lives in shoals; it is brightly coloured during the breeding season, especially the male which turns scarlet around its mouth, fins and belly. The minnow is a most inquisitive fish, and will even nibble at your fingers or toes if you dangle them in the water. A shoal will soon gather if there is any food about, and a piece of bright silver paper placed inside a minnow trap will soon catch some. Minnows are always on the move but must have clear and shallow running water to keep healthy.

Also living in the shallows is a bottom fish, the **Gudgeon**. It grows to about 20 cm, and is coloured grey or brown. Its underside is flat so that it can rest on the bottom, and its drooping face has a mouth with barbels. This fish also lives in shoals and seldom comes to the surface.

Where there are fish in rivers, there may be **Otters**. This shy and lovely animal is not easy to see as it is a great wanderer, mainly at night. Listen for its whistle, and look for its footprints. They may be found almost anywhere along a riverbank, seashore, marshland or reservoir.

otter with fish

perch

minnow

bream

gudgeon

dace

roach

stickleback

River Birds

Rivers contain fish, and this means that fishing birds will turn up wherever there is a chance of catching a meal.

A very patient and expert fisherman is the **Grey Heron**. Because of its long legs it can stand in shallow water without getting wet. Its long, curved neck rests on its shoulders as it watches and waits for something to pass by. This could be a fish, frog or water insect. Then, in a flash, out shoots the heron's long neck and its long, pointed beak spears a meal. Tossing the fish into the air, it catches it again and swallows it head first.

Being very shy birds, herons will only fish in quiet places, usually at dawn or dusk, and may take long journeys to reach their feeding grounds. They are not easy to approach. Even so, you may often see one from a passing train or car. They seem to be quite used to traffic, but not humans.

Every spring the herons return to their large nests in the tree-tops of the heronry, and repair them with fresh sticks after the damage caused by winter gales. They then lay their sky-blue eggs in them. When the youngsters hatch out, they make plenty of squawking noises as they demand food. You may also hear a curious clapping sound which happens each time food or nest material is passed from one bird to the other. This is done by throwing up the head and snapping the beak – a kind of "thank you" which is called the "receiving ceremony".

The sight of the beautiful **Kingfisher** is always a pleasure. Coloured a brilliant blue green above and chestnut below, it darts along the river like a living jewel, making for its nest which is merely a hole in the river bank. Usually it fishes from a stone or a branch hanging over the water. To catch a fish it dives straight in and brings back its catch which it then bangs against something to kill it. This small bird, only 15 cm long, can catch and swallow a meal which looks almost too big for its stomach. Sitting quietly by a river bank you may be lucky and see the

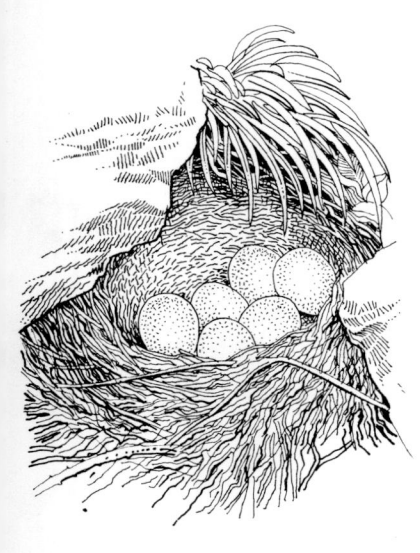

wagtail's nest

kingfisher at work. I was once angling by a lake when one actually flew across and settled on the end of my rod!

A strange song coming from the reeds, sounding like a jingling bunch of keys, could come from a **Reed Bunting**. About the size and shape of a sparrow, the cock bird has a black head and throat with a white collar and chest. The female is more brownish, and nests close to the ground.

Any birdwatcher would be pleased to catch a glimpse of a rather shy waterside bird, not all that common, which is related to the moorhen. It is called a **Water Rail** and is streaked in dark brown with black-and-white stripes down each side. Its beak is long and slender. The water rail skulks among the thick undergrowth close to water, and makes a curious sharp cry, sounding like "gep-gep-gep", mostly towards evening.

A bird which you may see tripping over the stones along streams and riversides, constantly bobbing its long tail up and down, could be one of the **Wagtails**. The **Grey Wagtail** is with us all year round, but the **Yellow Wagtail** is a summer visitor. The black-and-white **Pied Wagtail** is mostly seen on farms and in towns and villages. Wagtails feed on insects which they catch on the ground. You may sometimes see them where there are farm animals, such as cows, moving in the long grass. The animals disturb the insects and the wagtails catch them. These birds usually nest in holes in walls, bridges, rocks, or in river banks.

Warblers are small, rather drab, brownish birds with slender beaks which come over for the summer from Africa. Some of them, like the **Marsh Warbler**, haunt the riverside among the dense vegetation. You will probably first notice one by its loud and musical song which has many canary-like trills. Warblers can look so much alike that it helps to know their songs. Each one is different.

This small list of birds by the river shows once more how a habitat can be shared by many birds, each with a different way of living so that they do not compete with one another.

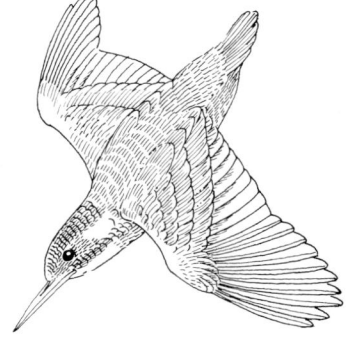

kingfisher

marsh warbler

kingfisher

reed bunting

grey heron

water rail

wagtail

The Salmon and the Eel

One of the largest and most handsome of our river fishes is the **Salmon**. Growing up to 90 cm long, it can weigh up to 25 pounds (12 kilos) or more.

The salmon is a fish of northern countries which travels upstream from the Atlantic to spawn in European rivers. This migration varies with different rivers, and may take place early or late in the season. It is a difficult and tiring journey, with many pauses on the way. There are dangers to face, such as the nets and fly-rods of the salmon fishermen, and also the otter and seal. Another danger is an eel-like creature, the **Lamprey**. It is a parasite with a sucker for a mouth which it can clamp onto a fish. It then feeds on the body with its rasping tongue, making nasty wounds. Then there are such obstacles as weirs and waterfalls to pass; it is a fine sight to watch the salmon leaping across these. During prolonged drought the water may become too shallow to pass, and from a bridge you can sometimes see salmon waiting patiently for some rain and deeper water.

Laying of the eggs takes place between September and February. The female, or **hen**, fish finds a clear and shallow patch high up the river where there is plenty of gravel and stones on the bed. Facing upstream, she turns on her side, and flaps her tail. This throws aside the gravel and stones so that a hollow trough is made. This becomes her nest, called a **redd**.

Meanwhile, the male salmon, or **cock** – he has a hooked lower jaw – is waiting nearby. The hen will lay up to 17,000 eggs which are then fertilized by the cock. Flapping her tail again, the hen then covers them up.

Here they remain all winter, hidden by the stones. Meanwhile, the exhausted parents, now called **kelts**, slowly drift downstream to the sea. Some die on the way, but others get there and soon recover their health and strength for another journey the following year.

In early spring the eggs hatch into tiny **fry** or **alevins**. They feed on their

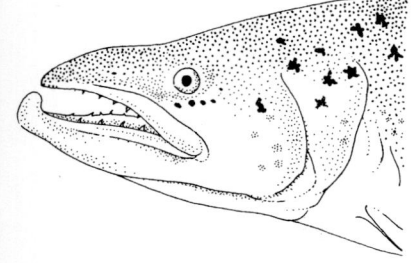

jaw of breeding cock salmon

bag of food, called the **yolk sac,** and can live on this for a while until they are strong enough to move about. This is called the **parr** stage, when they are beautiful little fish, marked with rainbow colours. The parr lives and hunts food near its birthplace for about two years.

Then a change takes place. The colours fade and it turns silver. It is then called the **smolt.** Now is the time for it to start its long journey down to the sea, where there is plenty of food and room to live and grow up. One day it will return as a mature salmon to lay its own eggs.

Another remarkable fish migration is that of the **Common Eel,** but here the story is reversed. The eel's birthplace is in the sea, and it lives and grows up in fresh water.

For years this was a mystery. People had always noticed that tiny eels would appear along the coast every summer, and make their way inland by way of rivers and ditches. Then, in autumn, numbers of grown eels were seen on their way downriver to the sea. Then they disappeared. What happened in between?

It was a Danish zoologist, Dr. Johan Schmidt, who found the answer. He used to go out with the fishing boats into the Atlantic to catch the small sea creatures which drift on the surface, called **plankton.** Among these was a curious animal with a tiny head, shaped like a willow leaf, which gives it its scientific name of *leptocephalus* (lep-tow-keff-a-lus). He noticed that these "tiny heads' became much smaller in size the further the boats sailed into the Atlantic. From this he realized that they were all the same creatures but of different ages and sizes. They were being carried across the sea in the currents, growing all the time.

Now the eel's secret is known. The adults migrate to the Sargasso Sea in the Atlantic and lay their eggs in the ocean. The *leptocephalus*, which is actually the larval stage of the eel, hatches out and is then carried on a journey of some 3,000 miles towards the European coast. As it reaches our shores, each larva turns into a baby eel, or **elver.**

adult eels

leptocephalus (larval stages)

cock salmon

hen salmon

redd

eggs

alevin

smolt

Dragonflies

Here and there during summer you will see **Dragonflies** darting about over the river. These handsome insects are quite harmless, yet some people still believe that they sting and bite, and even cause unpleasant things to happen, such as warts. This is all nonsense.

It would be far better to stop and watch their marvellous powers of flight, how they hover in the air, and even move backwards and sideways like a helicopter. You may even see one catch its prey in mid-air. As a fly, gnat, or even a butterfly passes by, the dragonfly pounces. In a moment or so the wings of its captive flutter down as the dragonfly bites them off with its powerful **mandibles**. It may then even eat its victim while still in the air.

In Britain there are about 40 different kinds of dragonflies, divided into two groups. The larger, more powerful ones are called **Mosquito Hawks**, and the smaller, more slender kinds are **Damselflies**. Apart from size and build you can also tell the difference by the way the wings are held when resting. A mosquito hawk keeps them spread out, looking like a miniature aeroplane, whereas a damselfly folds them along its body. There are differences, too, in the larval stage, which we shall see in a moment.

Mating of dragonflies takes place in the air, and you may see a pair passing by joined together. When they separate, the female starts to lay her eggs close to or even on the water. Eggs may be laid on water plants, or you will see a female bobbing up and down over the water. Each time the tip of her curled body touches the water surface, an egg is laid.

Each egg hatches into the larva, called a **nymph**. It has the usual insect number of six legs. The hawk nymph is thick set and has a pair of sharp mandibles fixed to a hinge which folds beneath its head. Creeping slowly

damselfly laying eggs in water

about among the underwater plants, it gets close to a tadpole, small fish, or even a newt. The jaw hinge, called a **mask**, shoots out, and the prey is captured.

This kind of nymph also has a hollow at the end of its body which can take in water. By forcing this out, the nymph can jerk itself forward in a kind of jet propulsion.

The slender and more delicate damselfly nymph can be recognised by its three "tails", which are really breathing organs. It swims by wriggling its body from side to side.

As each nymph feeds and grows, it sheds its skin, or **moults**, a number of times. If you search carefully among the water plants, you may find an empty skin looking like a ghost nymph.

Before the final moult the nymph crawls out of the water, up some reed stem or stick, and rests for a while to dry in the sun. The skin then splits along its back, and a dragonfly emerges. This may take nearly an hour. At first the wings are limp and crumpled, but soon they spread out as blood is pumped through the veins. Then, with a flash of wings, it is off, searching for food or looking for a mate.

By summer's end the dragonflies are mostly dead, but you could look for their empty larval cases still fixed to the reed stems by the riverside.

Dragonfly larva usually keep to the quieter backwaters of rivers, and can be found in ponds and lakes; they make good aquarium subjects. Give them plenty of water plants to cling to, and feed them on small water creatures, or little pieces of raw meat.

If you stand a stick in the aquarium or dish, you may one day be lucky to see your nymph crawl out and turn into a dragonfly.

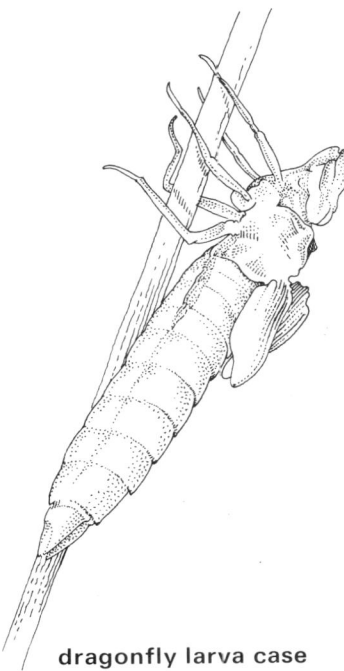

dragonfly larva case

125

dragonfly emerging

mosquito hawk adult

dragonfly emerging

mosquito hawk nyn
catching food

damselflies mating

mosquito hawk adult

damselfly nymph

Riverside Plants

A walk along the river bank is a good way of getting to know some of our wild flowers which like to grow in muddy places near water. Apart from the usual **Reeds** and **Rushes**, and trees like **Willows** and **Alder**, there are quite a few colourful flowers to look for. One of these is the **Water Iris** or **Yellow Flag**, a wild cousin of the garden iris.

After the flower has died down, hard, nut-like fruits appear which float away on the water. These may be carried miles down the river to lodge in another muddy corner, and grow into new irises. Also, by means of the underground stem, or **rhyzome**, this plant can spread along the riverside.

In spring the bright, golden yellow flowers of the **Marsh Marigold** or **Kingcup** appear. This is a cousin of the buttercup, and sometimes covers a whole meadow in a sheet of gold if the ground is damp.

The **Ragged Robin** belongs to the Pink family. It gets its name from its appearance, since the petals are deeply notched as if torn.

One curious riverside plant is the **Burr-reed**. What appear to look like small, prickly chestnuts are really clusters of small flowers. The lower clusters are male flowers which turn a bright yellow from the pollen they contain. The lower burrs of greenish, female flowers ripen into small fruits which also get carried away on water.

The **Spearmint** which we grow in our gardens to go with roast lamb has a relative called the **Water Mint**. Squeeze a leaf, and you can smell the same minty scent. Its lilac flowers grow in bunches on the end of the stalks.

The handsome **Purple Loosestrife** grows rings of bright reddish purple flowers on long stalks. It, too, likes a damp corner. Do not confuse it with the similar-looking **Rosebay**, one of the willow herbs which grows in dry places in towns or on burned ground.

reed mace discharging seed

Among the tall leaves of rush or reed-bed may be the club-shaped flowerhead on its long stalk of the **Reedmace,** sometimes wrongly called the **Bullrush.** The upper part is composed of tightly fitting male flowers which turn yellow when they ripen with pollen. Below this are the female flowers. By midsummer they have developed into tiny nut-like fruits, each with a tuft of white hairs. These are blown away by the wind. People sometimes gather these reedmace flower stalks, dry and paint them, and use them as house decoration.

One of the oddest looking waterside plants is the **Butterbur.** It looks a bit like a small pinkish cauliflower. On the stout, hollow stem is a cluster of flower heads. Some plants have only male flowers, other are female. The very large leaves may be up to 90 cm across, heart-shaped, resembling rhubarb leaves.

A study of wildflowers can be made more interesting by noticing the way they spread. Unlike animal babies, the seeds and fruits of flowers cannot move, so must be helped on their way. This can happen in a number of ways. Some are carried off by water, like the nut fruits of the Water Iris. Those of the Reedmace are blown away by the wind. Others spin through the air on wings, like the fruit of the Sycamore tree.

Here and there is a berry fruit, such as the hawberries of the Hawthorn, a common bush by the river. Birds eat this and digest the soft parts, but the seeds pass through their bodies. This may happen a long way away from the parent bush.

Some fruits have hooks which catch on to the fur of animals and on our clothing!

In these ways the plants are spread around the countryside, and many of them end up along the riverbank where there is rich mud and water.

water iris seed pods dispersing

burr reed

purple loosestrife

ragged robin

rush

water mint

butterbur

marsh marigold

water iris

reed mace

River Disturbance

It is a very sad fact that many of our rivers and streams in Britain have been upset or altered by man, and that this has disturbed or even killed off much of the wildlife.

In prehistoric times when there were few humans about, the rivers were clean and fresh, right down to the sea. Then, as more and more humans appeared, they made use of the river valleys where they could live a better and safer life, rather than stay among the trees in the dense forests.

The first people to do so were the New Stone Age or **Neolithic** farmers who came over from the Continent about 2,000 B.C. The great forests in those days made travel difficult as they were full of dangerous animals, such as wolves, bears and wild boar. The sheltered valleys seemed the best places to live in, where they could move about along the waterways in their boats. This, of course, was long before the days of roads and railways.

Crops could be grown on the rich valley soil, and their farm animals could feed and grow fat on the grass. There were fish and waterfowl to catch in the rivers and marshes, and reeds and wood to collect for making tools and household articles. In many ways living by the river was far better than trying to settle in the forest.

Most of our river towns and villages probably started in this way, and we still make use of the valleys. We make great use of the rivers, but at the same time we have done them a lot of harm. A journey down a river will show this.

Up in the hills or mountains the streams are still clean and fresh, and little disturbed except by an occasional fisherman after a trout, or a farmer and his sheep.

Lower down, among the foothills where the farms and villages begin to appear, there are fields of corn and grass. On this the farmer spreads his

discharging effluent

132

fertilizers to make them grow. Some of this may wash into the river. This can affect the life in an unusual way. Whereas the water plants may benefit from these chemicals, and grow rapidly, they also use up much of the oxygen in the water, and this can harm the fish and other animal life.

Another problem is caused by **sewerage**. This is the waste material which comes from our kitchen sink, bath, toilet, and from the drains in the road. It is all carried by pipes to the sewerage farm, and purified to make it harmless. However, the fine **sediment** which is left is sometimes poured into rivers. This **effluent** may cover and choke the water plants and even kill off the river life.

A far more serious danger can occur where a factory gets rid of its **waste products**. This kind of **pollution** could be anything from dirty water to a dangerous chemical.

Because of all these human activities, various oils, detergents, effluents and chemicals find their way into our rivers, and this does no good to the river life.

Then there is the general disturbance caused by **visitors** who like to go boating, swimming or fishing. Where there is a **port** or **docks**, large ships are constantly moving in and out.

Here and there we have built barriers like **weirs** and **locks**. In many rivers the banks have been steepened and the riverside plants cut back to stop flooding.

All this human disturbance is bound to have an effect on river life. Fortunately there are still many places where nature is doing her best to carry on as normally as possible. Attempts are now being made to try and clean up our rivers. Let us hope that it is not too late, for a day spent by a river in the quiet countryside away from noisy towns is something we can all enjoy.

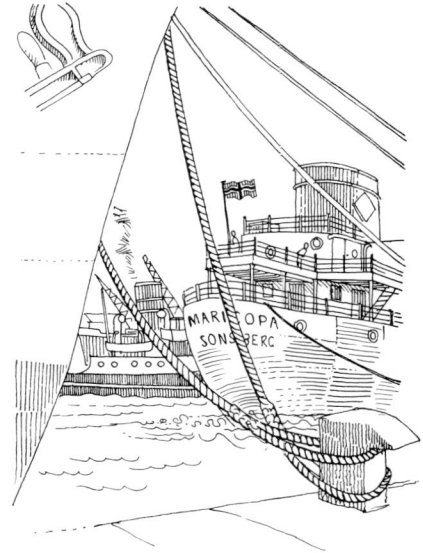

dockland

POLLUTION OF RIVERS AND WATERWAYS

CLEAN HEADLAND WATER
Young mountain stream containing fresh water, little disturbed by man

FARMING
Rich soil in river bends making good farmland. Fertiliser may be washed into river and upset the oxygen balance

RESIDENTIAL AREAS
Villages and towns in river valley. Here is a danger from sewerage damaging the water life

Index

(Illustrations are shown in italics)

Index
(continued)

1 pound	28·350 grams
1 ton	1016 kilograms
1 kilogram	2·2046 pounds
1 inch	2·54 centimetres
1 foot	0·3048 metre
1 yard	0·9144 metre
1 mile	1·6093 kilometres
1 metre	3·2808 feet
1 kilometre	0·6214 mile